GW00544576

BLAKE'S
FEAST

BLAKE'S
FEAST

A LIFE IN FOOD

ANDREW BLAKE

NEW
HOLLAND

First published in 2010 by New Holland Publishers (Australia) Pty Ltd
Sydney • Auckland • London • Cape Town

www.newholland.com.au

1/66 Gibbes Street Chatswood NSW 2067 Australia
218 Lake Road Northcote Auckland New Zealand
86 Edgware Road London W2 2EA United Kingdom
80 McKenzie Street Cape Town 8001 South Africa

Copyright © 2010 in text: Andrew Blake
Copyright © 2010 in images: New Holland Publishers (Australia) Pty Ltd & Andrew Blake
Copyright © 2010 New Holland Publishers (Australia) Pty Ltd

All rights reserved. No part of this publication may be reproduced, stored in a retrieval system
or transmitted, in any form or by any means, electronic, mechanical, photocopying, recording
or otherwise, without the prior written permission of the publishers and copyright holders.

National Library of Australia Cataloguing-in-Publication Data:

Blake, Andrew

Blake's feast : a life in food

  ISBN 9781741109580.

  1. Cookery.

  641.509

Publisher: Linda Williams
Publishing manager: Lliane Clarke
Food photography: Graeme Gillies, Simon Griffiths, Malou Burger
Cover photograph: Simon Griffiths and Graeme Gillies (top)
Project editor: Talina McKenzie
Proofreader: Nina Paine
Designer: Donnah Dee Luttrell
Cover design: Donnah Dee Luttrell
Production manager: Olga Dementiev
Printer: Toppan Leefung Printing Limited (China)

Acknowledgements

Blake's Feast: A Life in Food is a snapshot of my entire working life—34 years in restaurants and catering. Along with the lows that are well documented in this book, there have been many successes. Apart from my drive to succeed, I could not have achieved anything without the support of those close to me. The love of family and friends makes me a very happy person and has always meant I can bounce out of bed every morning with a purpose in my stride and I look forward to whatever the day may throw at me.

My mother Lenore has always given me love and unwavering support and her blind faith will be repaid in kind when I can finally return the title deed to her home that she put up as security a number of years ago. Her pride in me is painful but I have learnt to just accept it. My father Ron was absent for a number of my younger years, but by the time he died he had unknowingly imparted in me a sense of perspective: to just enjoy what you have while you have it. I hope that my son enjoys going to the football with me as much as I did with 'rotten Ronnie'.

To my first girlfriend Andrea who was an absolute gem when I was trying to find my feet as an apprentice.

To all my workmates and staff over the years who helped make work so much fun. There are too many to name and no one person any more important than the next.

A very special tribute to Gloria Staley who inspired me to be the best I could be, and to take pleasure in serving others.

To Glenby, who I have worked with for most of the last 30 years. We have a sometimes testy but enduring friendship and we will be able to look back and laugh at some of the things we have been through together.

I put my ex-wives Jennie and Mischee through all sorts of torment. To them I am grateful for their forgiveness and thankful for their roles in my career and the fact that I have stepdaughter Kasey, daughters Neredah and Claudette and son Jasper because of them.

To my great golfing mates Curls, Con and Grunter. Golf has been my therapy and outlet and you guys have made it all the more enjoyable. May our band never break up!

To my partner Jodie. How I ended up with someone that hates the foods I love I'll never know. But she has been great support through a period of serious rebuilding.

And finally to all my wonderful customers in the various jobs and businesses I have had over the last 34 years. Your appreciation of my cooking is all the encouragement I have ever needed.

Contents

Acknowledgements 05

The Menu 08

In the Beginning 12

A Lot to Learn
Apprenticeship 18
Fanny's 20

A Golden Era
The Metrolope & La Bouillabaisse 32
Fanny's—Second Time Around 33

Bright Lights
Chez Oz 44

The Sinking Ship
Arthur's 58

Reunions & Risotto
Café Kanis 78

25,000 Preserves
Kanis, Blake & Kanis 92

A Cinderella Story
Blake's 102

"You Know Nothing About Food!"
Stella, & Stella @ Heide 140

The Perils of Partnerships
Tonic 148
Events Warehouse 150

The Art of Making Tea
Blake's Cafeteria 166

Blake's Feast 196

The Menu

Canapes

crayfish club sandwich 203

fanny's quail-egg crouton sunnyside up 25

gazpacho shots with blueswimmer crabmeat
and basil oil 207

glo glo's hot cheese rolls 26

pea and prosciutto arancini, molten gorgonzola 208

peppered lamb fillet crostini, truffled
mushroom paté 216

quail saltimbocca on hummus crouton 204

ras el hanout spiced duck and quince mini pies 211

roast duck and pickled mango ricepaper rolls 215

Entrees, Sides & Salads

baked idaho potato filled with chorizo and
manchego 162

barbeque king prawns with a warm salad of baby
artichokes and white beans with rosemary oil 120

beetroot and vodka cured ocean trout with
goat's cheese fritters, soft herbs and sour cream 178

breaded calf's liver with silverbeet and gorgonzola 86

carpaccio of hiramasa kingfish, potato pancake,
cucumber and wasabi tobikko 63

chicken and coconut salad with smoked quail eggs,
chilli, peanuts and asian herbs 129

coulibiac of yarra valley salmon, chive beurre blanc
and salmon pearls 66

crayfish laksa, teardrop rice noodles, bean sprouts
and asian herbs 220

cream of celeriac soup with sage oil and
rabbit rillettes crostini 49

crisped zucchini flowers filled with porcini ricotta 212

gremolata crumbed buffalo mozzarella with
beet leaves, golden beets and hazelnuts 116

grilled squid and green mango salad 159

pan-fried barramundi with whipped taramasalata,
grilled salad onions and black olive oil 177

quail sausage roll with verjus sauce 145

real chicken noodle soup 99

rice noodle cannelloni of asparagus and
blueswimmer crabmeat with ginger-soy butter
and coriander-peanut pesto 119

sardine fillets in chickpea batter, tomato kasundi 156

sautéed duck livers with frisee, figs, cracklings
and blackberry vinaigrette 130

seared sea scallop tart with babagannouj and
basil oil 126

smoked salmon stack, pickled cucumber,
horseradish cream and lattice chips 123

steak sandwich with grilled artichoke, kipfler potato
and caramelised red onion 53

tarte tatin of olive oil poached tomatoes with
goat's cheese and green olive tapenade 71

tataki of sashimi tuna, soba noodles, shaved calamari,
shiitake mushrooms and snowpeas 219

thyme-roasted portobello mushrooms with brioche,
pecorino and pesto 174

wagyu beef chipolatas with bubble'n'squeak and
tomato jam 173

tuna tartare with pequillo peppers
and grilled sourdough 182

Conserves & Bases

coconut chilli jam 97

green tomato and apple chutney 96

master stock 99

parmesan oil 98

strawberry and rose petal jam 97

Mains

barbeque leg of milk-fed lamb with tzatziki and
a braise of baby fennel, tomato and olives 133

barbeque moreton bay bugs, sweetfish sauce,
mint and coriander 187

cassoulet of duck, lyonnaise sausage and
white beans 223

chermoula roasted kangaroo fillet, giant couscous,
silverbeet and tahini-yoghurt 134

chicken saltimbocca, puy lentils, cavalo nero,
truffled hollandaise 73

crayfish macaroni cheese with jalapenos 64

crisped king george whiting and fanny's chips 29

crispy skinned snapper, goat's cheese-mashed potato,
olive-red pepper-caper braise 85

geoff lindsay's crispy-skin duck with lup cheong,
bak choy and more chinese flavours 143

grilled boned quail, salad of shaved fennel,
grapes, figs and feta 157

grilled cotechino sausage with warm potato salad
and mustard fruits 125

hot and sour veal osso bucco 89

kentucky fried quail with vietnamese slaw 128

pan-seared red mullet fillets with wild rocket,
romesco sauce and grilled turkish bread 181

potato gnocchi, moreton bay bugs, sage brown butter,
peas and lemon 82

pumpkin tortellini with mustard fruits and
citrus butter 50

rabbit lasagne with tomato, sage and truffle-scented
béchamel 122

red peanut curry of twice-cooked lamb shank
with eggplant 160

risotto of lamb sweetbreads and broadbeans 70

roast rack of lamb, eggplant, anchovy and
buffalo mozzarella moussaka 115

snapper, mussel, leek and semillon pie 155

steak diane 39

whole deep-fried baby snapper with
three-flavoured sauce and root crisps 142

world's best-practice chicken schnitzel,
eggplant pickle 180

year of the goat curry 161

Desserts

apricot cheesecake 14

baby pavlova, strawberries, crystallised rose petals,
raspberry sauce and rose syrup 191

goat's milk and poached cherry créme brulée 54

hot passionfruit soufflé 40

individual quince tarte tatin 74

strawberry fritters, fig vincotto and sour cream
ice-cream 137

solomon island honey ice-cream sandwich
with gold leaf florentines 192

"Seeing people
enjoy my cooking certainly
gave me a buzz."

In the Beginning

I bought Mum a cookbook for Mother's Day way back in 1970. I don't know why I bought it but it was certainly more useful than the hand-cranked bread slicer that Dad bought her. Picture a small electric slicer you might see in a deli, but with a hand crank instead of a motor. Never saw her use it. But she still has that *Australian and New Zealand Complete Book of Cookery*.

Flicking through it recently made me realise how much cookbooks—and in fact food itself—have changed. Although a fabulous book in its time, very little in it would be appropriate these days. However, that book holds a special place in my cooking history: it contains the very first recipe I ever followed, my once-famous-with-Mum's-friends apricot cheesecake. Before that, my kitchen experience went no further than licking the beaters of the mixmaster when Mum had finished making a cake.

Seeing people enjoy my cooking certainly gave me a buzz. At the time it didn't make me think that I should consider a career as a chef, but it encouraged me to cook more. I didn't have a large repertoire, but I did enjoy making breakfast in bed for my parents on Sunday mornings. This consisted mainly of omelettes, though occasionally I served one of my dad's favourites, devilled kidneys. That might sound quite strange for breakfast, but Dad was a tradesman so meaty dishes such as breakfast steaks or lamb chops were not unusual at the breakfast table.

"At the time
it didn't make me think that
I should consider a career
as a chef, but it encouraged me
to cook more."

apricot cheesecake

Crush biscuits finely. Melt butter and add to the crushed biscuits with cinnamon and mix well.

Spread mixture over the base and sides of a 20cm (8in) springform tin and press firmly. Refrigerate for at least an hour.

Press the cheeses through a fine sieve, blend with vanilla essence and beat until creamy.

Beat eggs until frothy, then beat in sugar gradually until mixture is thick and foamy. Continue beating while adding the cheese in small portions, mixing each time until smooth.

Chop or mash six of the drained apricots and stir into the mixture.

Spoon into the biscuit base and bake at 150–160°C (300–325°F) for 35–40 minutes. Allow to cool in the oven with the door ajar.

Chop or mash the remainder of the apricots and add sugar and lemon juice. Blend cornflour with apricot syrup and add to the fruit.

Bring to the boil, stirring constantly, then simmer for a few minutes. Let cool and spread over the top of the cheesecake. Refrigerate overnight before serving.

250g (8oz) plain sweet biscuits (like teddy bears)
125g (4oz) melted butter
Pinch cinnamon
500g (1lb) cream cheese
250g (8oz) cottage cheese
1 teaspoon vanilla essence
4 eggs
1 cup sugar
1 x 900g (1lb 13oz) tin apricots
1 tablespoon sugar
1 teaspoon lemon juice
1½ dessertspoons cornflour
½ cup apricot syrup

"The first six months of my apprenticeship were the hardest... at times I did consider chucking the whole thing in."

A Lot to Learn

Apprenticeship

While waiting for the results from my Year 12 exams, I received a phone call from my uncle wanting to know if I was interested in a cooking apprenticeship. A mate of his was the house manager at a club on the outskirts of Melbourne.

Having been a lousy student with absolutely no desire to study any further, the idea of gaining a skill and being paid to do so was attractive. I accepted a trial period as an apprentice chef at the club. Mum bought me a set of knives and uniforms and I started on my eighteenth birthday. She was working so Nan drove me down with my suitcase packed to begin the next phase of my life. I had to live in at the country club as I had no driver's licence and, with a schedule of five split shifts per week, public transport was out of the question.

It was worse than I could ever have imagined. The staff quarters were akin to prison cells and my room was only just big enough to accommodate a single bed. There was a communal lounge for me to use but I had two fellow 'inmates', brothers that could have been extras from the film *Deliverance*. They worked as greenkeepers and got drunk in the lounge every night, so I spent my leisure time in my room.

I generally started work around 7.30am to help with breakfast. Once breakfast was cleared, lunch was readied for either bain-marie service in the bistro or for one of the many corporate conferences that the club attracted. I would finish work around 1.30pm and had to take a four-hour break, returning at 5.30pm for a short dinner service that saw me finish around 8.30pm. It was fortunate that I was permitted to play golf on either of the club's 18-hole championship courses because I was very much stuck on the premises. I soon gained my motorbike learner's permit and bought a bike that allowed me much more freedom. I would go home to Brighton for my days off. On some split shifts I would ride 30 minutes to Point Leo or Balnarring to bodysurf, which made the long day a bit more bearable.

The first six months of my apprenticeship were the hardest. The work seemed fine, but then I had nothing to measure it against. On weekends while I was working all my friends were going to the pub or parties or just going away as a group. I wasn't able to do any of this and at times I did consider chucking the whole thing in. My head chef was a little Napoleonic fellow from Manchester. I think he took it as his personal crusade to try and break my spirit. For two days a week I was kitchen hand while Kevin the dishy was on his days off; I was given all the worst cleaning jobs, had food thrown at me and copped plenty of mental abuse. Never once was I given a weekend off when one was requested. But the harder he pushed, the more resilient I became and the more determined I became that I would not give up this job, especially while this autocratic runt was my boss.

Apart from the fact that we were occasionally required to do so-called 'gourmet dinners', and that apprentices by law have to be trained by qualified chefs, the place did not really need a chef at all. The soups were made from bulk powdered bases, the vegetables were all frozen, the fruit was all canned and there was absolutely no love or care for anything that was handled in that kitchen. They were all good people, but they were just doing a job. And there was no-one there to teach me anything that would hold me in good stead in the future. But I deemed it important to finish my apprenticeship at the one establishment to show that I was reliable and loyal. And perhaps I was a little bit lazy, because if I'd been driven I certainly would have left at least a year earlier than I did.

Fanny's

A friend of my mum's had arranged an interview for me with industry legends Gloria and Blythe Staley for a junior chef position at Fanny's, one of Melbourne's top three restaurants at the time. The interview was to be conducted at Glo Glo's, a sister restaurant named after Gloria, located just off Toorak Village.

I went to Glo Glo's during my afternoon split shift from the country club. The day wasn't a classic Melbourne late winter one—it was incredibly bright and sunny. I was very nervous entering the restaurant, for the Staleys' reputation was formidable and I really knew very little about food or restaurant cooking.

Glo Glo's had no windows to the outside world, and without lights on it was like walking into a cinema: pitch black even in the middle of the day. I entered, and in the softly illuminated far corner sat the Staleys. I walked steadily towards them and after five steps crashed into a table, knocking off chairs that had been placed there for vacuuming after the previous night's service. I managed to stumble over another table and its chairs before reaching the Staleys, not daring to turn around to survey the carnage I'd left in my wake.

I can't remember that much about the interview—after all, it was nearly 30 years ago. But I believe it went along the lines of:

'Tell me Andrew, have you ever made a terrine?'

'No, Mrs Staley,' I nervously replied.

'Well, do you know how to make a bavarois then?'

'I've not made a bavarois before,' I stammered.

'How about puff pastry?'

'No,' I said, feeling even more inadequate.

'Well young fella, are you willing to learn?' piped in Mr Staley.

'Yes,' I confidently replied.

'Well, you can start in two weeks.'

I did start two weeks later, and what an eye-opener it was. I learnt more in my first three weeks than I did in my previous three years. I was one of two cooks working in the bistro downstairs along with a kitchen hand that washed up and made coffees. In the course of an average morning's prep, we would make stocks, ice creams, handmade pasta and sauces, break down whole cuts of meat into portions, fillet fish, prepare vegetables and make desserts. The bistro started to fill at noon, so you didn't start when you were rostered to: you generally started work an hour or more earlier to avoid 'getting in the shit' as we called it.

A couple of months later a car accident took the life of one of the restaurant chefs upstairs and maimed the bloke I cooked with downstairs. Taking the emotion out of it, losing a chef from a team at any time puts so much more pressure on everyone else in the kitchen. Take a chef from a brigade of five, and you have lost 20 per cent of your manpower. By losing my bistro companion, we were down 50 per cent! Gavin was replaced a couple of weeks later but not before I was racking up 15 hours a day, six days a week.

We had a great team of young chefs in those early days, all led by the inimitable Edouard Demanouf. In true Gallic fashion he would whack a couple of slabs of brie in a crusty baguette, make himself a large coffee, wait for the coffee to become tepid and dunk the brie-laden baguette in. He continually made the restaurant's demi-glaze in three hours. It may take the rest of us a day and a half, but Eddie as we not-so-affectionately called him would simply boil bones and meat, add port wine, tomato paste and blackjack, thicken it with cornflour and voilá!: almost instant demi-glaze.

I had always enjoyed cooking but only as a means to an end. I certainly became a lot more passionate about it at Fanny's. We worked hard and played hard, often going out clubbing or to see a band after work until the early hours, before letting ourselves back into the restaurant for a few hours' sleep on the banquettes in the bistro downstairs. The kitchen hand would come down to wake us and we would stagger upstairs, don the uniform and get cracking again.

My other great passion was football. I had always played through my schooling but falling into cooking did present some problems. During my apprenticeship I would work from 7am on a Saturday, finish at 1pm, race to whatever ground my team East Brighton was playing at before racing back to my job for a four-hour dinner service. Never had time for a shower; I just put my chef's uniform straight over the mud and cleaned up the exposed parts.

Changing the menus at Fanny's was an experience I would not want to go through again. Upstairs in the restaurant, the chef would sit with Mrs Staley for half an hour before reappearing with an armful of European cookbooks. Over the next couple of days he would send out her chosen dishes during our lunch service for her tasting and approval. This process would take place over a number of weeks until a menu had been finalised. All well and good, except the chef was the only person who knew what the hell was going on. So, come new menu time the first couple of services were always absolute bedlam. And there were no quiet services at Fanny's in the early 80s: they were full lunch and dinner on most days. I swore then that I would never change menus in this manner when I had autonomy over a restaurant.

Changing the menus in the bistro was even more diabolical. Often Mrs Staley would appear from nowhere with a clutch of cookbooks and say to me, 'Here is the menu, here are the recipes and here are they ways I want them to be presented.'

'When would you like the menu to start Mrs Staley?'

'Tomorrow will be fine thanks Andrew!'

So the bistro co-chef and I would do everything humanly possible to get everything ready for the next day's lunch. At midday, the bistro kitchen would have photocopies of recipes and photos plastered all over the small servery walls. Thankfully the customers were oblivious to our panic and somehow we always got through.

We had some great times and lots of fun. It helped make up for the poor pay. In summer we played laneway cricket between finishing our prep and waiting for the first customers to arrive. We would taunt men in trench coats grasping brown paper bags exiting the rear of two porno cinemas that shared our laneway. Once, our whole fruit and vegetable delivery, as always precariously balanced on the slippery external staircase, tumbled to the ground below. Trays of loose raspberries and strawberries went everywhere. The cool room was totally inadequate for the volume of food we used, so produce tended to stay on the staircase until it was required.

After coming from the under-skilled, uninspired kitchen of my apprenticeship, Fanny's was a revelation. For all I have described thus far, it was a wonderful experience. I loved my life at Fanny's bistro, but after two years it was time to head overseas. My only problem was money. I was getting $260 a week at that stage and there was no way that I was going to be able to save any money on that. It was time to leave and get a better paying job.

George Haddad,
waiter at Fanny's and Glo Glo's

"In summer we played laneway cricket between finishing our prep and waiting for the first customers to arrive."

Glenby and I, back of
Fanny's Restaurant (1980)

Fanny's

Sorbet à la Tomate 5.50
(Tomato Sorbet)
with
sauce au Vouvray 6.50
in a Vouvray sauce)
eau de saumon
th smoked

Feuil

Poire
(Pra

Poisson
(Poached

Sauté de Veau
(Sauteed Veal
crumbed and pan fried breast of
Suprême de volaille au beur
iquillettes de canard
Roast Duckling with a
Carré d'agn

fanny's quail egg crouton sunnyside up

Very lightly, butter both sides of the croutons and bake at 175°C (350°F) until golden brown.

Cut the kaiserfleisch into squares of approximately 2.5cm (1in). Crisp in a heavy fry pan over medium heat and place a square on each crouton.

Cut off the top third of the quail eggs with a small serrated knife and tip the eggs into the same pan. With a little oil, gently fry the eggs over a low heat.

When the eggs set, cut each with a 2.5cm (1in) round cutter. Top each 'bacon' tile with a sprig of flat-leaf parsley and then a quail egg. Season each with a small grind of black pepper and a little sea salt.

8 croutons, cut 5mm (¼in) thick
20g (²/₃oz) butter, softened
2 slices kaiserfleisch (smoked pork belly)
8 quail eggs
8 sprigs flat-leaf parsley
Black pepper and sea salt, to taste

glo glo's hot cheese rolls

Melt butter in a small saucepan and add flour to make a roux. Cook out over a low flame for a minute or two without colouring.

Heat milk, add a little to the roux and incorporate. Continue this process until you have a smooth white sauce. Add grated parmesan and cayenne pepper and season with sea salt.

Using an electric slicer, slice the loaf lengthways as thinly as possible, perhaps 2mm (1/16in). You should have approximately 20 slices that are around 20cm (8in) long and 10cm (4in) wide. Remove crusts from each slice.

Spread a thin amount of cheesy white sauce over each slice and roll up in to a cigar. Refrigerate the cheese rolls for at least one hour.

Heat oil to 170°C (340°F) and fry each 'cigar' until golden brown. Serve immediately.

¼ cup unsalted butter
¼ cup flour
2 cups milk
½ cup grated parmesan
½ teaspoon cayenne pepper
Sea salt, to taste
1 loaf white bread (unsliced and 1–2 days old)
1L (32 fl oz) vegetable or cottonseed oil

Although Fanny's was a top Melbourne restaurant spanning three decades, ask anyone who went there what their favourite dish was and invariably the reply will be 'the crispy fish and chips'. This isn't the way we cooked the chips then, but it is a very close adaption and a tribute to Gerry, the old fish cook at Fanny's who must have made 100,000 serves in his 20 years at the restaurant.

crisped king george whiting and fanny's chips

This batter is so simple but must be made as described for best results.

Mix the flours together in a bowl. Add beer and very gently stir in with a spoon. Add enough water to create a batter. Do not beat to get rid of lumps—let the batter sit for 30 minutes and the lumps will whisk out much more easily. Add a little more water if batter is too thick.

Heat cottonseed oil to 175°C (350°F).

While the oil is heating, trim the whiting fillets of any bones. Dust the fillets lightly in plain flour and then place in the bowl of beer batter, ensuring they are evenly coated.

When the oil reaches the right temperature, hold each fillet by the tail and gently immerse in the oil. Cook two fillets at a time, taking care not to drop them too early as they may splash hot oil and stick to the bottom of the fryer. Let the batter 'set' before letting go.

When the batter is golden brown, remove the fish from the oil and place on absorbent kitchen paper to soak up excess oil.

Peel potatoes and cut to 9cm x 1cm x 1cm (3½in x ⅜in x ⅜in). Cover with cold water and soak for 30 minutes to remove excess starch. Drain the chips well and pat dry with absorbent kitchen paper.

Heat duck fat to 130°C (260°F) and blanch the chips until just cooked and without colour. Drain and cool.

Heat cottonseed oil to 175°C (350°F) and cook the chips until golden brown and crisp. Drain well and season with sea salt.

Serve with lemon cheeks and your favourite sauce.

1½ cups self-raising flour
½ cup cornflour
375ml (1½ cups) pale ale
2L (64 fl oz) cottonseed oil
8 whiting fillets
1 cup plain flour
Lemon cheeks, to serve

chips
1½ kg (3lb) large Sebago potatoes
500ml (16 fl oz) duck fat
2L (64 fl oz) cottonseed oil
Sea salt, to taste

"I don't know whether my views were widely shared by the others, but I look back on this time as a golden era."

A Golden Era

The Metropole
& La Bouillabaisse

1982 wasn't the best of years personally. Though I had a great job at Fanny's and loved my football, I was hurting over a break-up with my first girlfriend. I would wallow in self-pity, lying on my couch listening to sad love songs in preference to going out. My old school mate Jonno suggested we go overseas. I purchased a one-way ticket to Europe to make the commitment, but still had to work out how to finance the trip. Easy, take two full-time jobs!

I left Fanny's 12 weeks before I was due to leave Australia and embarked on a massive savings campaign. I took a job with Denis Narcon, a fabulous pastry chef who was also the head chef at The Metropole in High Street, Armadale. I cooked six lunches a week from 7am until 3pm and then went to my second job at La Bouillabaisse. There I cooked for Gary Moore, six nights a week from around 3pm until 11pm.

La Bouillabaisse was very popular when it was run as a simple seafood restaurant by a couple of Greek guys. It featured a self-serve salad bar that was set into an old rowing boat and the customers loved it. When Gary bought the restaurant he removed the salad boat and, inadvertently, most of the old customers.

Neither The Metropole nor La Bouillabaisse were particularly stimulating jobs, but they served their purpose and I managed to squirrel away almost 10 grand for my European trip. The intention was to work in restaurants in Europe. The reality was that I had worked myself to a standstill doing around 95 hours a week for 10 weeks and had lost all desire to work there.

I saw and tasted much of Europe over the next four months, but returned to Melbourne when my mum asked me to come back. Her partner of four years had asked her to marry him and she wanted me there to give her away. I rushed back armed with a bottle of 1976 Taittinger Comtes de Champagne Rose that I had bought from the cellar door in Reims, ready to celebrate her marriage to George. As it turned out, I didn't need to be quite so hasty—they finally married four years later!

Fanny's Second Time Around

Even though I was lured back to Australia on the presumption I was giving my mother away, I was still very glad to be home. I had zigzagged all over Europe, utilising my Eurail pass very well by sleeping on trains, only occasionally enjoying the comfort of a bed. And my money was mostly spent.

One of the first things I wanted to do was go and see my ex-workmates at Fanny's. Climbing the filthy backstairs again for the first time in more than four months was eerie. When I left the restaurant I was looking forward to starting the next chapter of my life, but upon return realised that I did miss the place. It seemed like I had been away for years but comfortingly nothing had changed. It was very gratifying to be welcomed back so enthusiastically by the people I had worked with so closely before.

A position had only just become available in the upstairs kitchen and I guess timing is everything. I had lobbed on the restaurant's back door just as they needed a chef, the job was offered to me and of course I took it. Not because of the position and not for the pay—it was all about the people as individuals, the team we were part of and the camaraderie we had. It is hard to describe what we had and I don't know whether my views were widely shared by the others, but I look back on this time as a golden era. Later through my cooking life, I encouraged my young teams to strive for what I had enjoyed at Fanny's: to enjoy the companionship of the individuals that made up a great team, and to take great pride in what the team as a unit achieved.

Edouard left Fanny's and we all knew how he felt about us when his parting words were, 'I can't say that it has been a pleasure fellows!'

By this time Mrs Staley had started to involve most of the kitchen staff in menu development. Again, cookbooks were thrust upon us at relatively short notice. Along with the books, Mrs Staley would draw us diagrams of how she wanted the dishes to be presented. Sometimes she would bring out a sketch of a dish she had drawn at a three-Michelin-star restaurant in Paris. She knew what she was drawing but we had trouble seeing it!

The kitchen and machinery were kept clean, but it was old equipment in an older kitchen in an even older building. It was a very dark galley kitchen that was only used for service. Eventually the upstairs kitchen was renovated by order of the City of Melbourne Health Department. It was like all our Christmases had come at once for the long-suffering chefs.

Now, everyone knows that commercial kitchens are hot places. One summer the exhaust fans that sucked all the heat and smoke out through the canopy over the cooking equipment broke down. The motors were taken away to be rewired and we were without the exhaust system for three days through a typical Melbourne heatwave. Temperatures in the middle of service got to around 59°C and the smoke gave everyone extremely red and sore eyes. There was a collective cheer from the cooks when the servicemen came to install the rewired motors during our afternoon break. While we sought relief in a pub, the job was done. We got back to the kitchen and turned the fans on to discover the imbeciles had put the motors in upside down! Now the heat and smoke were being driven back into the kitchen. No servicemen to be seen and it was a Friday afternoon so we had to wait until Monday to have the job done properly. I would not wish anyone to go through what we did for those five days.

I don't have a superstitious bone in my body, but Fanny's sure had its fair share of tragedy. Apart from the accident early on that took the life of one and maimed another, accidents took other lives. Jacek was a young waiter from Poland who worked downstairs with Sammy. He was a wonderful person and I remember him very fondly. He would ask the kitchen for the discarded prawn heads so he could suck the gunk out of them. He invited me to his apartment to taste his homemade grappa that made his home look more like a distillery. Jacek got his motorcycle licence and was killed a couple of weeks later on a quiet country road. Castagna was my first kitchen lady at Fanny's Bistro and we worked together for a couple of years. She was an older lady and didn't speak a

Fanny's

Soupe glacée et sorbet à la Tomate 5.50
(Iced Summer Soup with Tomato Sorbet)

Feuilleté d'asperges et cervelles sauce au Vouvray 6.50
(Feuilleté of asparagus and brains in a Vouvray sauce)

Poire d'avocat, la mousse de truite son chapeau de saumon 7.50
(Avocado filled with a trout mousse and masked with smoked salmon)

Salade d'ecrevisse et bouquet, aspic de homard et mousseline de mangues 7.50
(Prawn and yabby salad with lobster in aspic and a mousseline of fresh mangoes)

Dodine de Cailles en gelée et son oeuf 7.50
(Stuffed boned quail in a port wine jelly with quail eggs and a watercress sauce)

Friture de crevettes et sa garniture 7.50
(Crisped Prawns and a lightly fried parsley)

Ragout d'huitres et de St Jacques et mousse aux truffes 7.50
(Ragout of oysters and scallops with a truffled mousse)

Gateau de vermicelle les rognons à la crême de bacon 6.50
(Vermicelle gateau with kidneys and creamed bacon)

Poisson du jour poché mousseline de concombres et menthe fraiche 10.50
(Poached fish of the day with a mousseline of cucumbers and fresh mint)

Crisped or Grilled Whiting 10.50

Sauté de veau au sabayon d'asperges 10.50
(Sauteed Veal with fresh asparagus)

Suprême de volaille au beurre de citron vert et gingembre 10.50
(Lightly crumbed and pan fried breast of chicken with green lemon and ginger butter)

Aiguillettes de canard au coulis de groseilles 12.00
(Roast Duckling with a coulis of red currants and grand marnier)

Carre d'agneau rôti aux artichaux 11.50
(Roasted baby lamb with julienne of fresh artichokes and new seasons vegetables)

Pigeonneau rôti au vinaigre de framboise 12.50
(Baked squab with raspberry vinegar sauce on a bed of fresh peas and bacon)

Filet de boeuf sauce au roquefort 11.50
(Fillet of beef with roquefort sauce and galette of potatoes)

"I encouraged my young teams to strive for what I had enjoyed at Fanny's: to enjoy the companionship of the individuals that made up a great team, and to take great pride in what the team as a unit achieved."

word of English, but understood what she saw and heard. She would natter on in Italian to me, well aware that my Italian was worse than her English. Castagna was run over and killed crossing the road. Gerry was more fortunate. Gerry was the fish cook and responsible for the famous crisped whiting and chips. Gerry was hit by a tram and was ill for a long time but survived.

Some time in late 1984, I was asked by the Staleys if I would like to move to Sydney to be the head chef at Chez Oz, their soon-to-be-opened restaurant in Darlinghurst. I discussed the idea with Jennie, my girlfriend of a couple of months. We were firmly entrenched in our relationship and I would only consider moving north if she came with me.

On a reconnaissance trip to Sydney to check out housing, other restaurants and schooling for Jennie's daughter Kasey, I suggested to Jennie that we should get married. We hadn't discussed the notion, but during a great dinner (and perhaps a bottle of wine) at La Strada, I made the suggestion. I know it doesn't sound very romantic, but the occasion demanded it. I am pretty sure Jennie accepted then and there.

The other thing the night was memorable for was the argument that ensued. Being a chef, I am always interested in the detail of other restaurants. Girardon cooking, or cooking at the table by waiters, is, thank God, a thing of the past. But it was quite popular in the mid-80s. I was trying to hold down my end of the conversation while watching our waiter deftly sauté my lambs' kidneys. Well, I was roundly berated for showing more interest in the waiter than in the conversation with my wife-to-be. And to think, she didn't even have the ring yet!

Chez Oz was to open in late August, so we married in early August, packed up shop and moved to Sydney.

steak diane

Between two plastic sheets, gently and evenly pound the fillet steaks flat so that they have a uniform thickness of a little less than 1cm (³⁄₈in).

Heat a large non-stick fry pan and wet with a little vegetable oil. Just before the oil smokes add the pounded minute steaks one at a time and sear both sides for around one minute before removing from the pan.

Add half the butter and sauté garlic and chilli for 20 seconds without colouring. Add Worcestershire sauce and when it boils add stock or demi-glaze.

Bring to a simmer and add spring onions. Reduce to a sauce consistency, remove from the heat and whisk in the remaining butter. Season with freshly ground black pepper.

A very small amount of cream can be added, but I prefer without. Place the steaks back in the pan with the sauce and simmer together for about 30 seconds.

Serve with mashed potato or fries.

4 fillet steaks of around 200g (6½oz) each, cut from the head of the eye fillet
Vegetable oil
50g (1¾oz) unsalted butter
2 cloves garlic, minced
1 chilli, finely sliced
100ml (3½ fl oz) Worcestershire sauce
200ml (7 fl oz) veal stock or
100ml (3½ fl oz) demi glaze
½ cup sliced spring onions
Black pepper, to taste
Cream (optional)

hot passionfruit soufflé

Bring milk to the boil.

Put egg yolks and sugar in a bowl and whisk until the sugar is almost dissolved. Add flour and whisk into the mixture. Add a small amount of the scalded milk and incorporate. Add half the rest and incorporate and then add the remainder.

Return the uncooked custard to the saucepan and heat slowly, stirring constantly until the custard thickens.

Place two tablespoons of the custard in a small saucepan with the partially strained passionfruit pulp and incorporate over a low flame.

Whisk egg whites with salt until they start to hold their shape. Add caster sugar and continue whisking until the sugar is dissolved and the meringue is stiff.

Fold the hot passionfruit mixture into the meringue and then spoon into four large soufflé cups that have been pre-buttered and dusted with caster sugar.

Bake at 200°C (400°F) for eight–10 minutes, dust with icing sugar and serve immediately.

175ml (5¾ fl oz) milk
2 egg yolks
50g (1¾oz) sugar
2 tablespoons flour
½ cup passionfruit pulp with
half the seeds strained out
6 egg whites
Pinch salt
200g (6½oz) caster sugar
Icing sugar

"A couple of huge boxes arrived from France containing 25 beautiful copper pots and pans.... I remember the joy of unpacking them, knowing I would have the privilege of cooking with them for the next couple of years."

Bright Lights

Chez Oz

Sydney was to be my watershed experience. I had been cooking for eight years and I had run shifts before, but Chez Oz was my first job as a head chef. I was 26 years old, but until now I had never wanted to be in charge of a kitchen. I hadn't felt ready for a head chef's position before. Too many young cooks finish their apprenticeships expecting to walk straight into a senior position, and some that do, make it. But many fall by the wayside, burnt out and lost to the industry. Young chefs have far too much to learn without the added pressure of being ultimately responsible for creating menus, staffing the kitchen, ordering produce and taking charge of the cooking that will decide the fate of the restaurant. Young chefs should be like sponges, absorbing everything they can from the chef they choose to learn from, then moving on to the next kitchen. Only when they feel they are well equipped with knowledge and maturity should they consider a head chef's position.

So I had done my time and I was ready. The Staleys asked me to delay my move to Sydney because Chez Oz was running a month behind schedule. I wanted to move straight there once I was married so we went ahead as planned, hoping to enjoy a couple of extra weeks to get to know Sydney before I started work.

One month became two, which finally became three before the restaurant was completed. I wasn't being paid at all during this period, and in the end I had to ask the Staleys for a week's salary because our money had been exhausted. We had been buying all our household needs on credit cards and enough was enough. The last delay, and the straw that broke the camel's back, was the owners deciding to repaint the entire restaurant. The difference in shade was negligible, but it put things back a further week.

The week leading up to our first night was interesting to say the least. The partners—Blythe, Gloria, their son Daniel, daughter Helen and her husband Malcolm—would come in the early evening for tasting sessions. It was the perfect scenario to get all the dishes fine-tuned. All was good in the kitchen, but not so good out front. I have never seen a family bicker and fight as much as I saw at these tastings. More than once, Malcolm left after having a glass of wine thrown in his face by Helen. Gloria was the matriarch of the family and always held court. I don't think the opinions of others were sought, and when they were offered they fell on deaf ears.

Before we opened, the family took me out for dinner a couple of times to check out the opposition. I don't know if Mrs Staley had a small appetite, but she only ever ate about a third of each dish she was served. I rather fancy she just loved messing with other restaurateurs' heads. On one occasion at Reflections, Peter Doyle's superb restaurant at Palm Beach, she thrust a menu to me under the table and whispered 'take this with you'. I am sure they would have given us a menu if we asked.

A couple of huge boxes arrived from France containing 25 beautiful copper pots and pans. The Staleys had ordered them from Dehillerin in Paris. I remember the joy of unpacking them, knowing I would have the privilege of cooking with them for the next couple of years.

We only had six people cooking at Chez Oz and all six worked the same shifts: Tuesday to Friday lunch and Tuesday to Saturday dinner. The place went off from day one and we had problems keeping up with the demand. For two years we were more or less full every service; it was the sort of place that Sydneysiders loved to see and be seen at. We were supposed to be working split shifts with a couple of hours off in the afternoon, but again ended up working straight through to replenish for dinner.

Chez Oz was inspired by Wolfgang Puck's Los Angeles eatery Spago: waiters in polos, jeans and white runners and an open plan kitchen with the chefs on full view. It was nerve-racking but had its advantages; I could see most tables in the restaurant and didn't have to rely on the waiters to let me know that a table was ready for their next course. Like Spago, we also had our fair share of celebrities. Rex Harrison and Claudette Colbert dined while they were playing in *Sweet Bird of Youth*. Elton John and Nick Faldo had lunch with the English cricket team when they were all on tour. And Stevie Nicks watched her entourage eat between regular visits to the powder room!

I was loving Sydney. When I could take an afternoon break, I would drive to Bondi or Tamarama and bodysurf for an hour or so. Jennie was pregnant and Chez Oz was rocking. In Melbourne, the chefs at Fanny's and Glo Glo's received very little recognition from the media: it was all about Gloria. But in Sydney I received much more publicity for my work, even though I was still cooking a menu constructed by Mrs Staley.

In 1986, the then federal treasurer Paul Keating introduced the Fringe Benefits Tax. Expensive corporate lunches were to become a thing of the past and the impact on city restaurants was immense. Jobs were lost as lunch trade was diminished. But Chez Oz didn't seem to be affected by the FBT. The restaurant was full every lunch,

Salad of marinated chicken with roasted peppers, papaya and green chilis.

Even the Chez Oz menu has the same bright, colorful look as its Los Angeles counterpart.

The cool, elegant uncluttered interiors and the kitchen open to the restaurant are all derived from the smart "glitzy" Spago's look, but done with such style one wonders why all restaurants don't have this feel. Its clean, crisp look is perfect for

the light, the climate and the snappy, smart arrogance that Sydney smacks of. However not everything has worked the way Helen anticipated. To her surprise the chefs didn't like the kitchen at first; it's in full sight of the diners, and they weren't used to being centre stage every night and having to hide every crisis. Now they love to feel part of the action and

certainly they have a box seat, viewing Sydney's glittering good-lookers eating their food with smiles of satisfaction. What could be more pleasing to a chef's heart.

Not that this is a surprise. Most of the dishes on the first menu (due to be changed every three months) have been pre-tested and pre-loved in either Fanny's with celebrities sitting next to Eastern Suburbs socialites. They in turn sat next to gangsters and standover men, who gambled between courses on the serial numbers of their wads of $20 notes! The dichotomies made for great viewing.

Menu changes at Chez Oz meant the Staleys would visit seasonally armed with recipes, cookbooks and diagrams. They would arrive on a Friday morning and on the Saturday I would have 15–20 specials ready to go from about 5pm, hoping and praying that we could bang them out before the evening's guests arrived. Somehow we arrived at a new menu and it was installed early the following week.

About a year after Chez Oz opened, my first child Neredah was born. Jennie's waters broke while we were having a cup of tea at home during a broken shift. I rushed back to work to arrange for my absence from the kitchen that evening and then took Jennie to hospital. Neredah was born four hours later.

I was overjoyed to be a father, but over the next year my marriage started to fall apart. I was in an industry that went out after work to wind down and I was out partying a couple of nights a week with other leading Sydney chefs. I knew it wasn't fair on Jennie or conducive to a healthy marriage, but I just didn't want to go home to a sleeping household. The temptations were too great and I was too weak to resist. The more I stayed out late, the worse our relationship became and that only made the decision to go out after work easier.

Glenby, my best mate from Fanny's, had moved to Sydney and, on my recommendation, had become head chef at the Four in Hand gastro pub in Paddington. We became good friends with owner Valdis and his business partner Paul Bard, and started talking about going into business together. The idea of finally being able to do my own food, in collaboration with Glenby, was appealing. Chez Oz had served a purpose, but it was time for me to move on.

cream of celeriac soup with sage oil and rabbit rillettes crostini

Dunk the whole bunch of sage into simmering water for 10 seconds to wilt. Plunge into ice water to refresh and pat dry.

In a bar blender blitz together the wilted sage and extra virgin olive oil. Transfer to a large jar and let flavours infuse for 24 hours, shaking vigorously every few hours. Strain through a fine sieve lined with muslin cloth and reserve.

In an ovenproof pot, heat flavoured duck fat and white wine. Chop the rabbit into eight or so pieces and immerse in the fat/wine liquid. Bring to a simmer, cover with a lid and cook slowly in an oven at 150°C (300°F) for two–three hours or until the meat is falling off the bone.

Carefully remove the rabbit from the liquid and pick the meat off the bones. Put the rabbit meat in a sterile jar and cover with fat. The rabbit rillettes should be refrigerated for a few days before use.

Sweat garlic and leek in butter for two minutes without colouring. Add diced celeriac and potatoes, cover with chicken stock and simmer until the celeriac and potatoes are tender.

Puree with a stick blender. Add cream and season with sea salt and ground white pepper. Pass through a strainer. Serve the soup hot with a drizzle of the sage oil.

Toast slices of baguette and top each with a spoonful of rabbit rillettes. Serve on the side.

1 bunch sage
500ml (16 fl oz) extra virgin olive oil
500ml (16 fl oz) flavoured duck fat
250ml (8 fl oz) white wine
1 rabbit
2 cloves garlic, diced
1 leek, diced
50g (1¾oz) butter
1kg (2lb) celeriac, peeled and diced
250g (8oz) potatoes, peeled and diced
1L (32 fl oz) chicken stock
150ml (5¼ fl oz) cream
Sea salt and white pepper, to taste
4 slices baguette cut 1cm (³⁄₈in) thick

pumpkin tortellini with mustard fruits and citrus butter

Combine pumpkin in a bowl with ricotta, parmesan, one tablespoon mustard fruits and one egg. Mix well and season with sea salt and freshly ground black pepper. Refrigerate.

Place flour and salt in the work bowl of a food processor. With the motor running, add eggs one by one, finishing with olive oil. Stop motor as soon as incorporated. Turn mixture out onto a workbench and knead for five minutes into a smooth dough. Wrap in plastic wrap and rest for 30 minutes.

Divide the dough into three balls. Roll a ball through a pasta machine on the thickest setting. Fold into three and roll through again. Repeat this laminating process until a smooth dough forms. Now gradually reduce the setting and roll until the pasta has gone through the thinnest setting. Cut the pasta sheet with an 8–10cm (3–4in) dough cutter, stacking up the pasta circles to prevent drying out. Cover the stack with plastic wrap and repeat the process with the remaining two balls of pasta dough.

Place a small tablespoon of filling in the centre of a pasta circle. Brush the edges lightly with eggwash and fold into a half moon, pressing the edges down well to create an airtight pocket. Hold a point of the pasta pocket between your thumb and little finger and wrap the half moon around your little finger, joining the two points and pressing together to form a tortellini. Repeat the process with all remaining pasta circles.

Cook the tortellini in gently boiling water for two minutes. Remove and place in a wide pan with lemon juice over a low heat. Add butter a couple of cubes at a time, gently swirling the pan to incorporate the melting butter and prevent the tortellini sticking. Do not boil the sauce as it can very easily separate. Season with a little sea salt and freshly ground black pepper.

Spoon tortellini onto serving plates and garnish with the remaining mustard fruits and shaved parmesan.

1 small pumpkin, baked and flesh mashed to yield 250g (8oz) pulp
100g (3½oz) ricotta cheese
60g (2oz) grated parmesan
3 tablespoons coarsely chopped mustard fruits*
1 egg
Sea salt and black pepper, to taste
250g (8oz) flour
1 teaspoon salt
3 eggs
2 tablespoons olive oil
Eggwash
50ml (1¾ fl oz) lemon juice
125g (4oz) unsalted butter, cut into cubes
½ cup shaved parmesan

* Mustard fruits are an Italian product of fruits preserved in syrup that has been flavoured with mustard seeds. They are available at good delis and providores.

steak sandwich with grilled artichoke, kipfler potato and caramelised red onion

Melt butter and sweat red onion over a medium/low heat for five minutes. Add red wine, red wine vinegar and sugar and cook for another five–10 minutes until the liquid becomes syrupy.

In a bowl, whisk together egg yolks, mustard and white wine vinegar. Slowly drizzle in the olive oil to form a mayonnaise. Add horseradish and stir in well. Adjust seasoning to taste.

Trim artichokes of tough outer leaves. Simmer artichokes in lightly salted water until the heart is tender. To test this, insert a small pointy knife where the bulb meets the stem. When tender, refresh the artichokes in cold water.

Remove the tough tips, cut into eighths lengthways and remove the 'furry' choke. Brush artichoke pieces lightly with oil and grill on a ribbed grill plate or barbeque for 45 seconds each side. When cool, cut these artichoke pieces into two or three smaller pieces.

Simmer kipfler potatoes in lightly salted water until tender. Cool and peel the skins off. Cut the kipflers in half lengthways and then in 5mm (¼in) slices. Mix the potato crescents and artichoke pieces in a bowl and add enough horseradish mayonnaise to just bind.

Roll the whole piece of beef tenderloin in a hot pan with a little oil to seal on all sides. Place on a baking rack on an oven tray and cook slowly at 140°C (275°F) until the centre of the meat is 50°C (120°F). Remove from the oven and cool. When cold, wrap whole piece of beef tightly in three–four layers of plastic wrap.

Cut the beef into 1cm (⅜in) thick slices and remove the plastic wrap. Place a slice of rare tenderloin on the centre of each plate. Top with caramelised onion and a thin layer of potato and artichoke mixture. Place another slice of tenderloin on top to create a 'steak sandwich'. Surround each steak sandwich with dressed young leaves.

75g (2½oz) unsalted butter
1 red onion, finely sliced
100ml (3½ fl oz) red wine
2 tablespoons red wine vinegar
1 tablespoon caster sugar
3 egg yolks
1 tablespoon Dijon mustard
3 tablespoons white wine vinegar
400ml (13 fl oz) olive oil
3 teaspoons grated fresh horseradish
2 globe artichokes
250g (8oz) kipfler potatoes
1 x 600g (1lb 3½oz) piece beef tenderloin (off a small fillet)
50g (1¾oz) young mixed leaves

goat's milk and poached cherry créme brulée

Simmer water, red wine, cinnamon stick and sugar together for five minutes. Add pitted cherries and poach for five minutes. Remove cherries from liquid and cool.

Preheat oven to 150°C (300°F).

In a saucepan, heat goat's milk, cream and vanilla bean to just below simmering temperature. Take off the heat and remove the vanilla bean. Scrape the seeds from the pod and return both to the liquid.

In a bowl, whisk egg yolks and sugar together. Add the hot liquid to the whisked yolk mixture. Let custard cool and then strain.

Place six or seven poached cherries in each brulée dish and cover with custard. Stand dishes in a baking dish and fill to halfway with water. Cook in the preheated oven for about 45 minutes. The brulées should be set around the outside and slightly wobbly in the centre.

Using a wire sieve, shake a thin layer of caster sugar over the brulées. This will disperse the sugar evenly and guarantee an even caramel top. Carefully caramelise the sugar layer under a very hot grill or with a blowtorch.

200ml (6½ fl oz) water
200ml (6½ fl oz) red wine
1 cinnamon stick
½ cup sugar
400g (13oz) cherries, pitted
180ml (6 fl oz) goat's milk
350ml (12 fl oz) double cream
1 vanilla bean, split lengthways
7 egg yolks
100g (3¼oz) sugar

Arthurs Restaurant Potts Point

Oysters with cucumber dressing & Sevruga caviar

Nicoise soup · a rich tuna broth with beans, tomato, quail eggs & a tapenade crouton

Sweetbreads on a fennel & onion marmalade with a mild chilli butter

Baked goats cheese salad with dried figs

Smoked ocean trout & avocado fuillette with chive cream & tomato vinaigrette

Terrine of roasted red, green & yellow capsicums with a lambs tongue, watercress salad and olive bread

Char-grilled bugs with saffron noodles, leeks & mussels

Charred leg & breast of duck with a spinach, turnip & duck liver tart

Quails stuffed with vegetables and served with wild mushroom ravioli

Chicken pan-roasted with garlic & rosemary, gratinéed artichokes & creamed potatoes

Beef & three veg!

Grilled John Dory on a tomato & ginger sauce creamed leeks & asparagus

Picatta of veal & veal liver with gorgonzola spatzle & ratatouille

Lamb chops with grilled vegetables, potato gnocci & basil orange jelly

Rhubarb souffle with apple & cinnamon ice-cream

"Death by chocolate"

Mandarin brulée with fruits poached in champagne

Macadamia & framboise parfait

The Sinking Ship

Arthur's

Arthur's was a legendary place in Potts Point in the 1980s. Famous for having Dolph Lundgren as a doorman while his girlfriend Grace Jones was living in Sydney, it was run as a very successful nightclub by Arthur Karvan. That is, until they lost their licence. The liquor licensing police had a telephone book-like document of infringements and misdemeanours against them and determined that not only was Arthur Karvan unfit to hold a liquor licence, the very building that housed Arthur's was to be banned from being a licensed premises.

I didn't know Arthur Karvan but I received a phone call from him in 1988 just after he lost his licence. A meeting ensued at his Victoria Street restaurant (incidentally, served by his budding actress daughter Claudia) and we talked about the possibility of me leaving Chez Oz and moving to Arthur's, which had now become an unlicensed restaurant. Nothing came of the meeting, but by coincidence Valdis and Paul from the Four in Hand hotel bought the building a couple of months later with intentions of resurrecting it as a licensed restaurant.

For all our combined knowledge of food, Glenby and I knew nothing about real estate. We presumed that Valdis and Paul had made a good decision in purchasing the property, a decision made on advice from their lawyers that we would be able to get the building and our business re-licensed. That was the first mistake. It took more than six months and $80,000 in legal fees to get a licence and had they known, Valdis and Paul may not have made the purchase in the first place.

The other mistake was the financing. It was 1989, and we were in the middle of 'the recession we had to have'. Interest rates were at 18 per cent and the business was confronted with an interest-only loan repayment of around 20 grand a month. That was an incredible burden to expect a restaurant charging 1989 prices to meet. I was oblivious to this until some time later. All I knew was that I was excited to be doing my own thing for the very first time.

Arthur's was on the city side of Victoria Street which fell down sharply towards Woolloomooloo Bay. Street level was actually the middle of five split levels, with the kitchen in the basement. There was a magnificent rear courtyard one level down from the entrance with huge, shady plane trees and an uninterrupted view of the city skyline that at dusk was silhouetted by the setting sun.

The building was very run-down. I remember being in Arthur's nightclub one evening when plaster started falling off the ceiling due to the dance floor above buckling under the strain. The building was thoroughly renovated to bring it up to restaurant standard and we opened with a cocktail party for around 300 invited guests. A couple of our girls painted a black birthmark under the left eye of every guest on arrival, a tribute to former owner Arthur Karvan, who had a very distinctive birthmark there. Jenny Kee once said it gave him the look of a panda bear.

We were all full of hope. The Sydney restaurant scene had been flat for a while and we thought the time was ripe; we had an iconic site and a talented kitchen. We were wrong. We fought hard to beat the difficulties that conspired against us by coming up with what we thought were smart solutions, but they didn't work. And some of our decisions were just bad.

Firstly, we didn't change the name. Everyone knew where Arthur's was, so why change the name? The trouble was, everyone also knew what Arthur's stood for, and trying to sell it as a serious restaurant was a major mistake. Secondly, parking was a real issue. We were told by potential guests that they had driven around trying to find a park, then given up and gone elsewhere. Victoria Street was full of backpacker hostels, which gave colour to the area but also clogged up the streets. Every backpacker had a van or car for sale and took up all available street spaces. So we offered a subsidised valet parking service, which helped a little but became horrifically expensive.

Then there was the small matter of the liquor licence. After opening it became apparent that we were not going to get the licence very soon. So we put together a wine list of bottles that were available from the bottle shop of the Piccadilly Hotel some 100 metres up the road. We presented the wine list to our patrons and upon ordering, the waiter sprinted up to the pub, purchased the bottle and sprinted back. The whole exercise was hilarious in its audacity and execution. If nothing else, it showed that we were creative in our endeavour to get over any hurdles.

On top of this, Arthur's' rear courtyard backed on to a laneway that was a favourite haunt for junkies. In the 12 months I was there we had four junkies tagged and bagged. On one occasion, David threw some fruit at a man to get him to move along from a fire escape that was in full view of any patrons on the glass-walled fourth level. He didn't move and soon enough the telltale appearance of bodily fluids told us that he wouldn't be moving under his own steam. Forgive me if I sound callous, but working around the Cross and Darlinghurst for almost four years does harden you to scenes like this.

Glenby and I came up with a menu concept for Arthur's that may have been inspired by a meal Jennie and I had at Ménage à Trois in London. A couple of friends had worked for Anthony Worrell-Thompson and suggested we go to his Beauchamp Road restaurant while passing through England on a whirlwind holiday. We met Anthony and he suggested that rather than ordering, he would send out a selection of dishes for us to sample. A great meal of small dishes followed and we invited Anthony to have a glass of wine with us at its conclusion. He came out of the kitchen with a hand swathed in bloodied tea towels and said that he would be back as soon as he had a couple of fingers stitched!

Our menu at Arthur's was made up of 20 or so savoury dishes of the one size: a bit bigger than an entrée and much smaller than a main. The idea was that three of these dishes would be the equivalent of an entrée and main at roughly the same cost. It was a very liberating experience creating our own menus and relatively successful, at least from a critical perspective. Some customers got it and loved what we did, ordering 12 different dishes to share for a table of four. Others felt uncomfortable without an entrée/main concept.

Oh, I've got another theory as to why Arthur's didn't work. Not a major theory, more another lame excuse, but I will run it by you anyway. There was a widely held belief at the time that Sydneysiders dined to see and be seen. As diners at Arthur's were spread across two floors, two mezzanines and a courtyard, there were no more than 25 guests on any one level. No matter how dexterous you were, it was impossible to see with any voyeuristic detail other diners on other levels. And that made people-watching very difficult.

About seven months after Arthur's opened, Jennie left me and returned to Melbourne with Kasey and Neredah. My behaviour and general disdain towards our marriage must have been intolerable and I don't know how she put up with me for as long as she did. I did love her but I was so absorbed in my own cooking and partying life. I was probably far too emotionally immature to be married in the first place. The day her father arrived with a removalist's van to pack up all the furniture was a very difficult one. Yes, I had created the whole situation but coming to the realisation that I wouldn't see the girls every day was a bitter pill to swallow.

After a tearful farewell with the girls, I went back to work. There, my day got worse. Glenby was upset with me for not being at work, an argument ensued and I ended up punching him in the nose—a difficult thing to do properly as he was standing at the stoves and I was on the other side of the pass, with a couple of food warming shelves between us. With nose bloodied, he snatched his apron from around his waist and threw it on the floor. Glenby understandably stormed out of the building so I picked up his apron and finished whatever he was cooking.

Later I found him at The Midnight Shift, one of his favourite gay haunts. Not a bad place to apologise either: there were blokes hugging everywhere so I didn't feel too conspicuous, although doing it under a mirror ball did seem a tad shallow.

Arthur's was not trading well and as a result I wasn't being paid much money. I quickly discovered that going home to a sleeping household was much better than going home to an empty one. I didn't have the phone switched on so I had to arm myself with $10 worth of 20-cent pieces and talk to my daughter at a public phone box around the corner. I missed my family terribly, life was difficult and Sydney had lost its shine.

I didn't feel good leaving a sinking ship, but I was going nowhere and had to get out.

carpaccio of hiramasa kingfish, potato pancake, cucumber and wasabi tobikko

Place potatoes whole and in their skins in lightly salted water and simmer until tender. Peel while they are hot and put into the bowl of a food processor.

With the motor running, add milk. Add the egg and egg whites one at a time until a smooth batter is formed. Add flour and season with salt and pepper.

Cook a small pancake in a non-stick fry pan to test the 'set'. If right, cook four pancakes of about 10cm (4in) in diameter, moistening the pan with a little oil between batches.

Peel cucumbers and finely slice. Salt the cucumbers well and set in a sieve to drain for 15 minutes.

Rinse off the salt and pat cucumbers dry. Mix with yoghurt and tobikko and season with a little freshly ground black pepper. Spoon the cucumber mixture onto the potato pancakes.

Slice the raw kingfish as thinly as possible with a very sharp knife. Lay the kingfish over the cucumber, top with a drizzle of lemon-flavoured extra virgin olive oil and sprinkle with micro herbs. Sprinkle with a little sea salt and serve.

250g (8oz) potatoes
250ml (8 fl oz) milk
1 egg
2 egg whites
40g (1½oz) plain flour
2 Lebanese cucumbers
½ cup Greek-style yoghurt
2 tablespoons wasabi tobikko
Black pepper, to taste
300g (10oz) Hiramasa kingfish (from the fattest part of the fish)
60ml (2 fl oz) lemon-flavoured extra virgin olive oil
4 tablespoons mixed micro herbs
Sea salt, to taste

crayfish macaroni cheese with jalapenos

Bring milk to the boil and remove from heat. In a saucepan, melt butter and stir in flour over a low heat to form a roux. Add milk a little at a time to the roux, stirring constantly.

Once all the milk has been incorporated, add cream, mustard and raclette. When the cheese has melted, add jalapenos and chives. Season and keep warm.

Boil macaroni in a large pot of lightly salted boiling water until barely cooked. Drain the macaroni and add to the cheese sauce.

Cut crayfish into thumb-sized chunks and add to the macaroni cheese. Spoon into four gratin dishes and bake in a hot oven (200–220°C, 400–420°F) for five minutes. Serve immediately.

300ml (10 fl oz) milk
40g (1½oz) butter
40g (1½oz) flour
½ cup cream
2 teaspoons Dijon mustard
200g (6½oz) grated raclette cheese
3 tablespoons sliced jalapeno chillies
3 tablespoons chopped chives
300g (10oz) macaroni
1 cooked crayfish of around 750g (1½lb), meat removed

coulibiac of yarra valley salmon, chive beurre blanc and salmon pearls

Dissolve yeast in the tepid water. In another bowl, dissolve salt and sugar in milk. Place in the bowl of an electric mixer with a dough hook attachment.

Add flour and then the yeast solution. Beat for two minutes then add four eggs, continuing to beat until the dough is smooth. Add the remaining eggs one at a time.

Increase the speed and beat for a further five minutes.

Lower the speed and add butter in small chunks. Mix until completely incorporated.

Place the dough in a large bowl, cover with a cloth and leave at room temperature for two hours to prove.

When the dough has doubled, knock it back. Cover and place in the fridge for another two hours until it has once again doubled in size.

Knock the dough back again and refrigerate overnight.

Remove all the pin bones from the salmon fillet with tweezers or pointy-nose pliers and skin completely.

Cut a 20cm (8in) long section off the thickest part of the fillet. Trim the thin rib flap off so that you are left with a piece of salmon about 6cm (2⅜in) wide. Wrap the salmon in a nori sheet, trimming any excess seaweed.

Place 300g (10oz) of the salmon offcuts along with the smoked salmon offcuts in the work bowl of a food processor. Run the motor for five-10 seconds before adding the egg whites. When they have been incorporated and the mixture is smooth, add cream and quickly mix in.

Place the salmon mousseline in a bowl, season and refrigerate.

Place the wrapped salmon fillet on a clean chopping board. Using a palette knife, apply an even 5mm (¼in) thick layer of mousseline on the top. Cover the mousseline with a single layer of smoked salmon slices. Cover the whole fillet with a sheet of plastic wrap and invert.

Repeat the process of spreading the mousseline and covering with smoked salmon. The fillet should now be wrapped in a layer of nori, followed by a layer of salmon mousseline then a layer of sliced smoked salmon. Enclose in plastic wrap and refrigerate.

Preheat oven to 210°C (410°F). On a floured bench, roll out the brioche to a 5mm (¼in) thickness and in a shape that will enclose the entire fillet in one piece of brioche.

Place the salmon fillet on the dough and carefully remove the plastic wrap. Fold over the sides to completely enclose the salmon, trimming any excess brioche where necessary.

Turn the unbaked loaf over so the brioche join is on the underside. Place on baking paper on a baking tray and tuck the brioche ends in to tidy and properly seal the fish in.

Lightly brush with eggwash and leave for 20 minutes in a warm part of the kitchen. Bake for 10 minutes before turning down to 190°C (375°F) for a further 15 minutes to finish.

While the coulibiac is baking, make the beurre blanc. In a small non-corrosive saucepan, bring wine and lemon juice to the boil and simmer for 10 seconds. Remove from the heat and whisk in cold butter a little at a time, returning to the heat occasionally to maintain the temperature. Be careful not to boil or simmer as the sauce can easily separate.

Add salmon pearls and chopped chives to the warm beurre blanc and adjust seasoning to taste.

The coulibiac is ready when the brioche is nicely browned and the inside cooked, not doughy. The fish should be warm and translucent, not opaque.

Cut the coulibiac in half through the middle and cut 2cm (¾in) thick slices from the centre out. Discard the ends as the fish normally overcooks there. Serve the coulibiac on warm plates and spoon the beurre blanc around the fish.

brioche
3 teaspoons fresh yeast
2 teaspoons tepid water
2 teaspoons salt
2 tablespoons sugar
2 tablespoons milk
470g (16½oz) flour
6 eggs
450g (16oz) unsalted butter, room temperature

salmon fillet
1 fillet Yarra Valley salmon (or any premium salmon)
1 nori sheet
150g (5oz) smoked salmon offcuts
3 egg whites
100ml (3½ fl oz) cream
10 slices smoked salmon
Eggwash

beurre blanc
2 tablespoons white wine
2 tablespoons lemon juice
160g (5½oz) cold unsalted butter, cut into cubes

garnish
30g (1oz) salmon pearls (roe)
3 tablespoons chopped chives

coulibiac of yarra valley salmon,
chive beurre blanc and salmon pearls

risotto of lamb sweetbreads and broadbeans

Soak sweetbreads in a large bowl of ice water for two hours, changing the water after one hour. Pull off and discard any fat and sinew.

Bring a pot of salted water to the boil and add vinegar and sweetbreads. Simmer for two minutes. Remove pot from the heat but leave the sweetbreads in the pot for a further 20 minutes.

Drain and plunge sweetbreads into a large bowl of ice water to cool. Drain, pat dry, and set aside. Clean any remaining connective tissue and cut into 1.5cm (⅝in) chunks.

Remove broadbeans from their pods and simmer in salted water until tender. Remove and discard the outer skins.

In a non-stick pan, sauté onion and garlic with olive oil and unsalted butter without colouring. Add arborio rice and sauté a further minute, again without colour. Add 250ml (8 fl oz) hot stock and simmer until almost absorbed. Add a similar amount of stock and repeat the process.

Add stock as required until the absorption process starts to slow and the rice bloats somewhat. The rice is ready when it is firm but not crunchy, and soft but not mushy.

Remove the pan from the heat and add the sweetbreads and broadbeans, tossing to warm gently. Add grated parmesan and season with sea salt and freshly ground pepper.

500g (1lb) lamb sweetbreads
2 tablespoons vinegar
300g (10oz) broadbeans
1 onion, chopped
2 garlic cloves, minced
75ml (2¾ fl oz) olive oil
25g (⅘oz) unsalted butter
350g (11½oz) arborio rice
1L (32 fl oz) chicken or white veal stock, hot
75g (2½oz) grated parmesan
Sea salt and black pepper, to taste

tarte tatin of olive oil poached tomatoes with goat's cheese and green olive tapenade

Core tomatoes, cut through the middle lengthways and gently squeeze out water and seeds. Place in a small baking tray or saucepan with whole garlic cloves and cover with olive oil. Roast in the oven for one hour at 70°C (160°F).

Remove the tomatoes and garlic from the oil, cool and remove the tomato skins.

Wash basil and immerse the whole bunch in simmering water for five seconds to wilt. Pat dry and blitz in a food processor with the oil from the tomato poaching.

Chop olives, capers, anchovies, minced garlic and parsley by hand to a coarse paste. In a small bowl, wet the paste with a little of the basil oil.

In a 12cm (4¾in) roesti pan, arrange three half tomatoes cut side up and three half cloves of garlic. They should fit snugly. Top with a puff pastry disc so that 1cm (⅜in) of pastry overlaps the tomatoes. Repeat the process in three other pans. Bake at 200°C (400°F) for 10–12 minutes, or until the puff pastry is cooked.

Invert each tatin, place a disc of goat's cheese in the centre and top with a small quenelle of green olive tapenade. Drizzle the tatins with a little basil oil before serving.

6 small ripe Roma tomatoes
6 garlic cloves, peeled
1L (32 fl oz) extra virgin olive oil
1 bunch basil
100g (3½oz) pitted green olives
1 tablespoon small capers
2 anchovies
½ teaspoon minced garlic
2 tablespoon chopped parsley
4 puff pastry discs of 12cm (⅛–¼in) thick
4 x 2–3cm (¾–1¼in) diameter rounds of goat's cheese

chicken saltimbocca, puy lentils, cavalo nero, truffled hollandaise

Soak lentils overnight. Rinse the lentils off and cover with plenty of fresh cold water in a saucepan. Add salt and simmer over a low heat until tender. Refresh and set aside.

In a small pan, sauté shallots in butter for one minute. Add sugar and caramelise, continually tossing the shallots. When caramelised, add water and simmer until the juices are syrupy and the shallots tender. Add a little more water if further cooking is required.

Place vinegar, wine, onion, bay leaves and peppercorns in a small saucepan. Simmer until the liquid is reduced by three quarters.

Strain the liquid into a bowl, add egg yolks and whisk over a double boiler until the mixture thickens to form a sabayon (a foamy sauce). Take care not to overcook the sabayon and 'scramble' the egg yolks.

Gradually add warm clarified butter to the sabayon, whisking well as you go. Finish the hollandaise with truffle oil and adjust seasoning to taste.

Place two sage leaves on each chicken breast and wrap in two slices of prosciutto. Sear the chicken breasts evenly in a heavy pan with a little olive oil. Transfer the wrapped breasts to a wire rack on a baking tray and cook for 20 minutes at 160°C (325°C).

While the breasts are cooking, sauté cavalo nero in a little butter in the chicken pan for two minutes without colouring. Add the lentils and sauté a further two minutes. Add the caramelised shallots and demi-glaze and cook for a further two minutes. Adjust seasoning to taste.

Share the lentil mixture between four plates. Cut each chicken breast crossways on a slight angle and into three pieces. Place cut side up on the lentils and nap with truffled hollandaise.

200g (6½oz) Puy (French green) lentils
1 teaspoon salt
12 red shallots, peeled
30g (1oz) butter
2 tablespoons sugar
125ml (4 fl oz) white wine vinegar
125ml (4 fl oz) white wine
1 small onion
2 bay leaves
1 teaspoon black peppercorns
2 egg yolks
200ml (6½ fl oz) clarified butter
1 teaspoon truffle oil
8 sage leaves
4 chicken breasts
Olive oil
8 very thin slices prosciutto
1 bunch cavalo nero (Tuscan black cabbage), cut into fine shreds
150ml (5¼ fl oz) veal demi-glaze

individual quince tarte tatin

Place sugar, water, cinnamon, lemon juice, squeezed lemon and vanilla bean in a heavy non-corrosive saucepan. Bring to a boil and turn down to simmer for five minutes.

Peel and core quinces and place in saucepan. Quince quarters should be submerged. If not, submerge by weighing down with a small plate or saucer. Cover with a lid and place in an oven set at 140°C (275°F). Cook for two to three hours until tender and deep orange–red in colour. Cool.

Heat four small roesti or blinis pans (approximately 12cm (4¾in) in diameter) and put three tablespoons of sugar and one tablespoon of butter in each. Heat pans over a low-medium flame until the sugar caramelises then remove from the heat. Add a couple of tablespoons of water to each to stop the caramelisation.

Cut the quince pieces so that the chunks can be packed tightly into the pans, preferably skin/round side down. Cut puff pastry into rings the same size as the pans and place over the pans on top of the quince chunks.

Heat oven to 200°C (400°F) and bake the four individual tatins for 20 minutes or until the pastry is golden brown, crisp and cooked through. Invert the pans and carefully remove the tatins while they are hot. Use a spatula if necessary to help dislodge the quince.

Plate, pouring over any excess caramel, and serve with a jug of pouring cream at the table.

500g (1lb) sugar
1L (32 fl oz) water
1 cinnamon quill
1 lemon, juiced (keep lemon)
1 vanilla bean, split
2 quinces
12 tablespoons sugar
4 tablespoons butter
1–2 sheets ready rolled butter puff pastry
Pouring cream, to serve

Reunions & Risotto

Cafe Kanis

When I came back to Melbourne in May 1989 I had no idea where I might cook. My confidence was high even though Arthur's was a failure—as I explained, there were many contributing factors. My mate Tony Marron had moved to Melbourne and bought Khyat's Hotel in Brighton. His chef was in need of a holiday so I covered for him while he was away.

Now, some people will accuse me of having a selective memory but this could not be further from the truth. I just cannot remember how Jennie and I got back together but any which way, it was great to be back with my family. I had been extremely reckless during the five months we were apart and it was reassuring to have some stability in my life again.

I phoned Virginia Hellier, a well-known Melbourne food consultant, to see what jobs were around. She said I should take a good look at a smart new café in Richmond, Café Kanis. I sat in my car outside for an hour or so over two evenings to watch the movement and get a feel for the place. I ate in the café and was disappointed by the food, which was perfect—now I could go into an interview knowing that Café Kanis needed me.

Virginia arranged a meeting for me with the owners, the Kanis cousins John and John (we used the terms 'Fair John' and 'Dark John' to differentiate between the two). Both Johns came from restaurant families, but this was their first foray into hospitality if you discount pulling beers in the family pub. They had been open for a couple of weeks and had recognised that the food wasn't doing justice to their investment.

Towards the end of our meeting, I remember Fair John asking me what sort of remuneration I was after. I said straight out, $800 a week net, because cooks always talk net. None of this gross annual stuff because most cooks are incapable of calculating what would end up in their hand each week. Before I answered, John was leaning forward with elbows on the table. When I gave him the figure I wanted, he took a deep breath and sat back on the banquette to ponder. I think it may have been more than Fair John had been led to believe a chef would cost, but Dark John knew exactly what a good chef was worth to his new business and the deal was done.

Café Kanis was designed by Stuart Rattle, a friend of dark John's. A high ornate plaster ceiling gave the café a voluminous feeling. Chequered black and white tiled floors, chocolate brown banquettes, large bevelled edge mirrors down both long walls and a huge antique railway clock over the bar were standout features. I loved the look of Café Kanis and felt it was a good fit for me.

There is a fantastic family history to the building. It had been owned by the Kanis family since the two Johns' grandfather Mick ran the Kanis Oyster Café on the very same site back in the 1930s. During renovations, some old Oyster Café menus were found behind an old wall and showed that back in the 30s chicken was more expensive than crayfish. Oh how I long for those days! The story also goes that the Richmond Football Club would have lunch at Kanis Oyster Café on a Saturday, then walk down to Punt Road Oval to play. How things have changed.

The kitchen was new, but the equipment was old and rudimentary: a six-burner stove with oven under, a char grill, a deep fryer and a salamander. Our plate-up bench opposite the cooking equipment had a hot box under and no refrigeration. This meant we had to walk 30 feet to get food from the cool room to cook: a situation that is totally unsatisfactory for any kitchen and one that suggested the money had almost run out before the café was completed. With some not-so-subtle prompting, the equipment was upgraded with under-bench refrigeration and even a Carpagiani ice-cream machine, which was a bit of a luxury for a café.

A risotto featured on every menu for the two years I was at Café Kanis. I certainly wish I knew then what I know now. Any risotto I have made in a restaurant or café in the last 18 years has used blanched rice so it only takes five or so minutes to finish and serve. For the first couple of months I could have three or four pans of risottos on

Dad, Neredah, myself, brother Davo & Kasey (1987)

"I can't believe that when an order came in for a risotto, I went through the whole process... Before too long I discovered the joys of using blanched rice and I never looked back."

Four generations: Nan O'Callaghan, Mum, myself & Neredah (1987)

the stove at any one time at various stages of their 21 minutes of cooking time. I can't believe that when an order came in for a risotto, I went through the whole process—chopped onion and minced garlic sweated in butter and olive oil, before adding rice and then stock followed by the hero ingredient and finishing touches. Before too long I discovered the joys of using blanched rice and I never looked back.

Café Kanis had two very different faces. By day, the tables were unclothed and it was more of a casual drop-in-for-a-coffee-and-snack-while-shopping or quick-lunch type of place. By night, the pendant lights were dimmed, the tables were clothed and the room had a much more refined feel.

I had cooked a couple of times for Melbourne restaurant legend Ronnie DiStasio at Chez Oz in Sydney and I remember the evening he came in to Café Kanis for the first time. On the menu we had an entrée of three different caviars that were served with steamed tiny new potatoes, sour cream and an oyster shooter. Ronnie enjoyed it so much he ordered a second serving. The idea was to eat the caviars and then down the oyster shooter. One customer, unsure of how to tackle the dish, proceeded to pour the shooter over the caviars before eating the lot. I was glad I didn't see it happen.

My behaviour towards my marriage had started to deteriorate once again. When driving home from Café Kanis after the evening shift, I often came to the proverbial fork in the road. Do I veer left to go home or right to go to Redheads, one of my favourite places to go for a drink and a game of pool?

potato gnocchi, moreton bay bugs, sage brown butter, peas and lemon

Wash potatoes, place in a large saucepan whole with skins on and cover with cold water. Bring to the boil and simmer until tender. Drain and peel while hot using rubber gloves if necessary.

Place peeled potatoes on a clean workbench and mash with an old-fashioned potato masher. Add half the flour and work into the potato. The idea with gnocchi is to use the starch in the potato as much as possible to hold the gnocchi together, not the starch in the flour.

Test the gnocchi by taking a small piece of dough and dropping it into lightly salted simmering water for one minute. If the gnocchi is not binding, add more flour and repeat the testing process until you are satisfied with the result. Season with salt and ground white pepper.

Roll out the gnocchi to form a 'sausage' 2cm (¾in) in diameter. Cut into 2cm (¾in) sections and cook in boiling water.

When cooked, remove gnocchi to a bowl of iced water. Cool, drain and lightly oil to prevent sticking. Store on a tray until required.

Melt butter in a large pan. When foaming, add bugtails and sauté for two minutes.

Remove from the pan with a slotted spoon, lower the heat and add the gnocchi. Cook for four minutes, tossing occasionally.

Turn up the heat and add sage. When the butter starts to turn a nut brown colour, add peas, chilli and lemon zest and continue to toss.

Add back the bugtails and toss for 20 seconds. Season with sea salt and freshly ground black pepper and serve.

800g (1¾lb) potatoes
200g (6½oz) flour
Salt and white pepper, to taste
100g (3½oz) unsalted butter
12 bugtails, meat removed from shell whole
2 tablespoons chopped sage
½ cup cooked peas
2 small chillies, deseeded and finely sliced
Zest of 1 lemon, finely grated
Sea salt and black pepper, to taste

crispy skinned snapper, goat's cheese-mashed potato, olive-red pepper-caper braise

Scorch the red pepper by placing it whole on a naked flame on the stovetop. As the skin blackens, rotate periodically to scorch the whole pepper evenly. This process should take around five minutes.

Place the scorched pepper in a small bowl and cover with a cloth for five minutes. Peel the skin off completely under running cold water. Cut the pepper into 7mm (¼in) dice. Dice the pitted olives to a similar size.

Put the red pepper dice, olive dice, baby capers and extra virgin olive oil into a small saucepan over low heat. Braise together for about five minutes, allowing the oil to bubble gently, not violently. Remove from the heat.

Simmer potatoes, with their skins on, in lightly salted water until tender. Drain and remove the skins while they are still hot.

Mash the potatoes with goat's cheese and enough goat's milk to make a smooth creamy mash. Season with sea salt and ground white pepper and keep warm.

Preheat oven to 200°C (400°F). In a large heavy pan, place the snapper fillets skin side down in olive oil and cook for about two minutes over medium/high heat. Turn the fish over and place the whole pan in an oven for four–five minutes depending on the thickness of the fillets. When the fish is cooked, remove from the oven.

Serve the crispy snapper fillets on a base of goat's cheese mash and spoon around the warm pepper braise.

1 large red pepper
½ cup Kalamata olives, pitted
2 tablespoons baby capers
200ml (6½ fl oz) extra virgin olive oil
6 medium-sized potatoes
100g (3½oz) goat's cheese
150ml (4¾ fl oz) goat's milk
Sea salt and white pepper, to taste
75ml (2¾ fl oz) olive oil
4 x 200g (6½oz) pieces snapper fillet

breaded calf's liver with silverbeet and gorgonzola

Tear the bread, crust and all, into large chunks. Blitz in a food processor to make coarse breadcrumbs. Do not overprocess.

With the calf's liver on a chopping board smooth side up, make a small, shallow incision with a small knife to break the skin. Remove the skin by deftly running your index finger between the skin and the flesh to separate them. Slice liver on a 30-degree angle from the horizontal and about 4–5mm (1/8–1/4in) thick. Only slice the top half of the liver as the lower half contains veins and arteries that we want to avoid. You should get 12 good thin slices from one 600g (1lb 3½oz) liver.

Lightly flour each slice of liver, dip in the beaten egg and then into the breadcrumbs to coat.

Heat the cream, demi-glaze and gorgonzola gently together in a saucepan over a low heat until the cheese has melted. Set aside.

Heat the olive oil and butter together in a non-stick pan until the butter starts to foam. Cook the breaded calf's liver in the foaming oil until golden brown. Turn over and cook the other side to golden brown.

Heat the gorgonzola cream mixture and add silverbeet. Simmer until the cream mixture has a sauce consistency. Spoon onto plates and top with two or three slices of the pan-fried calf's liver.

1 loaf of day-old bread
1 calf's liver
1 cup plain flour
1 egg, beaten
300ml (10 fl oz) cream
100ml (3½ fl oz) veal demi-glaze
100g (3½oz) gorgonzola
50ml (1¾ fl oz) olive oil
25g (⁴/₅oz) unsalted butter
½ bunch silverbeet, stalks removed and coarsely shredded

hot and sour veal osso bucco

Place shallots, garlic, chillies, turmeric and water in a food processor and blitz to a paste. Rub into the osso bucco and marinate for six hours.

Bring tomato paste, tamarind, palm sugar, lime leaves, lemongrass, galangal and veal stock to the boil and pour into a roasting tray. Add the marinated osso bucco, cover with foil and cook in an oven at 200°C (400°F) for 50–70 minutes until tender. Cooking time will depend on how young the osso bucco is.

Remove veal from the roasting pan. Strain the braising liquid, reduce to a sauce consistency and adjust seasoning to taste. Serve osso bucco in the strained sauce with mashed potato.

6 shallots
6 cloves garlic
3 birds eye chillies
2 tablespoons grated turmeric root
50ml (1¾ fl oz) water
1kg (2lb) veal osso bucco
150ml (4¾ fl oz) tomato paste
100g (3½oz) tamarind, wet to a paste and passed through a fine sieve
45g (1½oz) palm sugar, shaved
6 Kaffir lime leaves
1 lemongrass stalk, chopped
1 galangal knob, sliced
500ml (16 fl oz) veal stock
Mashed potato, to serve

25,000
Preserves

Kanis, Blake & Kanis

In 1988, Jennie and I visited Dean and Deluca on Broadway in New York City. Dean and Deluca was the closest thing I have seen to a department store for foodies and I spent hours wandering the aisles, marvelling at the quality of the produce, the sheer quantity of lines and the beauty of their merchandising displays. While there are many great food retailers in Australia (Jones the Grocer, Leo's, Fratelli Fresh) and around the world (Fauchon, La Grande Epicerie du Bon Marche), none has the range and depth of this Manhattan landmark. The cookbooks, cookware, super fresh seafood, meat and poultry, prepared meals, bakery and fromagerie guarantee you will buy more than you really need and spend more than what is in your pocket.

I returned to Australia with the dream that one day I would open a little version of Dean and Deluca. In my spare time I quietly developed a product range that would form the basis of a food retail outlet.

I spoke to the Kanis boys about the concept and the possibility of going into partnership with them. We thought South Yarra was probably the best location because there were more potential customers in the area with more disposable income. Dark John's father located a couple of sites and we decided on a shop in Toorak Road where a pharmacy was ending its lease.

The shopfront itself was around 50 square metres. This didn't give us a huge amount of space to work with, but it was better to have a small space generously stocked than a larger space that looked stark and lacking in product. We worked with Stuart Rattle, who had done such a great job on Café Kanis. A couple of layouts were developed and Stuart applied our preferred layout to his French Provencal design.

Next we needed a name. I thought it might be a bit of fun to use our three names, giving the business a name that was more akin to a law firm. So Kanis, Blake & Kanis was born.

We didn't want Kanis, Blake & Kanis to be known as a deli or providore. The French term 'traiteur', which translated to 'caterer', fitted our business better and it suited the look and feel of the place.

I started production a couple of weeks before we were due to open and learnt as I went along. I had studied up on the art of preserving and as everything was produced and packaged by hand, it was very labour intensive. All glass containers had to be sterilised. If I had a combi-steamer it would have made the process very easy, but all I had was a 100-litre stockpot full of boiling water. The glass jars were immersed in the boiling water for five minutes, then removed with a wire spider and placed upside down on a wire rack. When drained, the hot product was ladled into the jars using a wide-neck funnel and the sterilised lid was screwed on. The filled jar was immersed in water just below simmering point for 21 minutes. The jars were then removed, generally clumsily, with the wire spider and lids finally checked for tightness. This process was both time-consuming and painful. I developed calluses from hand-tightening very hot lids on very hot jars and would estimate that around 25,000 preserves were made each year.

We also made stocks, including chicken, fish, veal and the derivative demi-glaze. We even made quail stock when we had quail bones stockpiled from Café Kanis. There were always 12 or so soups available from the freezer at any time as well as a wide range of our own ice-creams and sorbets. Packaged home meal replacements such as lasagnas, curries, shanks and casseroles were stocked in the self-serve upright fridges. Pestos and tapenades were staples, along with sweet condiments such as berry sauces and citrus curds. The display cabinet was always filled with salads or vegetable dishes.

The only things we bought in were cheeses and smallgoods. Everything else was made on the premises, quite often at a loss because I sometimes just made things on a whim, like some filled pasta that I would take to a mate's business six kilometres away to vacuum-bag for sale, or some quail eggs that I would hard-boil, give a crackle tone effect to and preserve for display in the cabinet. Both a waste of time and money, but they used skills I enjoyed practising.

"Everything...was made on the premises, quite often at a loss because I sometimes just made things on a whim."

Staff at Kanis, Blake

One of the best things we did was employ pastry cook Loretta Sartori. Not that we could afford her, but she knew her worth, and her pastry work was beautiful. Loretta made the suggestion that we should wholesale her product 'so she could pay her way'. It worked to a point, but financially the business was a slog. The Johns and I worked without pay when things were at their tightest. KBK was a good idea badly timed; Australia was still in recession and we were not earning the revenue we forecast.

My marriage had been struggling right through the two years we had KBK. I remember going to the bank with Jennie to arrange finance for our share of the set-up costs. It was a terrible day and one that I will never forget, if only for the look of disgust on her face. Jennie was doing this for me even though deep down she knew she didn't want to.

Jennie was working full-time and I had had no income for a year. I had to leave KBK and get a job. John Van Handel had bought The Stokehouse a couple of years earlier with his brother Frank and was a good customer at KBK. I accepted the job of running downstairs at The Stoke while also doing hours at KBK. On Saturday and Sunday mornings I would start cooking at KBK at 3 or 4am to get the food prepared for the cabinet before going to The Stokehouse at 10am for a 12-hour shift.

Mandy Egan managed the shop for us, and her sister Kerry, or Kegs as she was affectionately known, worked on the weekends when we were very busy. I was invariably knackered on Sunday mornings, and Kerry suggested I would benefit by taking her Tenuate diet pills. I didn't need to lose weight, but they certainly did the job. I would literally race through my Stokehouse shifts, where we would do around 500 for lunch before having to prep up for dinner and do it all again. But what goes up must come down, and I would feel terrible on Mondays.

green tomato and apple chutney

On a low heat, sweat brown onions, garlic and ginger in vegetable oil until softened but not coloured. Add green tomatoes, green apples, all spice, cider vinegar, brown sugar, mustard seeds and currants. Bring to a boil and reduce heat to simmer for 40 minutes.

1kg (2lb) brown onions, peeled and diced
5 garlic cloves, chopped
1 knob ginger, minced
100ml (3½ fl oz) vegetable oil
2kg (4lb) green tomatoes, diced
1kg (2lb) green apple, diced
4 teaspoons all spice
300ml (10 fl oz) cider vinegar
300g (10oz) brown sugar
3 tablespoons yellow mustard seeds
100g (3½oz) currants

strawberry and rose petal jam

Wash strawberries well, hull and cut in half. Mix well with sugar and lemon juice in a non-corrosive saucepan and let sit for 15 minutes.

Bring the mixture to a boil and simmer for 10 minutes, skimming off the impurities as they rise and foam. Remove from the heat and stir in rose petals. Store in the refrigerator unless you choose to preserve.

1kg (2lb) perfectly ripe strawberries
500g (1lb) jam sugar (with pectin)
Juice of 1 lemon
2 cups scented pink or red rose petals, washed

coconut chilli jam

Heat safflower oil to 170°C (340°F) and fry shallots and garlic in small batches until crisp and golden. Drain on paper towel.

Fry dried shrimp and chillies for 30 seconds and drain.

Place all these ingredients in a food processor and blitz into a paste, adding 250ml (8 fl oz) of the cooled safflower oil to thin.

Place the paste in a saucepan and bring to the boil, adding tamarind water, palm sugar, salt and fish sauce. Simmer for five minutes.

Place coconut cream in a saucepan and reduce until it starts to split. Add the chilli jam and cook for a couple more minutes over a low heat. Use to flavour stir-fries.

750ml (24 fl oz) safflower oil
250g (8oz) red shallots, peeled and finely sliced
125g (4oz) garlic, peeled and finely sliced
½ cup dried shrimp
5 dried long red chillies
100gm (3½oz) tamarind, wet to a thick paste and passed through a fine sieve
125g (4oz) palm sugar
1 tablespoon salt
2 tablespoons fish sauce
500ml (16 fl oz) coconut cream

One of the oils I used to bottle and sell at Kanis, Blake & Kanis was a parmesan oil, which Teague Ezard once confided in me had inspired him to create his parmesan and garlic oil. My oil requires no grated parmesan cheese as I have seen in more recent parmesan oil recipes. Just lots of parmesan rinds, which can be difficult to accumulate, unless of course you work in a busy café/restaurant!

parmesan oil

In a heavy non-corrosive saucepan, heat the rinds and oil on as low a heat as possible for around six hours. At no time should the oil be too hot to dip your finger in. Heating excessively tends to break down the fruitiness of the oil. Let cool and strain 24 hours later.

Parmesan rinds
Enough extra virgin olive oil to cover them

real chicken noodle soup

Wash chicken and pat dry, removing any excess fat. Place in a large pot with carrots, onion, celery, garlic, peppercorns and bay leaves. Add 15L (480 fl oz) cold water and bring to a boil. Skim and simmer for one hour.

Remove the whole chicken and replace with chicken carcasses. Return to a boil and gently simmer for two hours, skimming as necessary.

Strain the stock. If you want a stronger broth, then continue simmering the strained stock until it has reduced to your desired strength. Season with sea salt and plenty of freshly ground black pepper.

Remove the chicken meat from the bones and shred. Add to the soup with the risoni and chopped parsley.

1 whole chicken
2 carrots, peeled and chopped
2 onions, cut in half, cut side blackened in a hot pan
2 sticks celery
2 garlic cloves
1 tablespoon black peppercorns
2 bay leaves
1kg (2lb) chicken carcasses
Sea salt and black pepper, to taste
1 cup risoni, cooked
¾ cup chopped flat-leaf parsley

master stock

Put all ingredients in a saucepan and simmer gently for 30 minutes. Let stock and ingredients steep for a further 30 minutes and strain.

* Yellow rock sugar is available at most Asian grocers.

2L (64 fl oz) chicken stock or duck stock
200ml (6½fl oz) Shaoxing wine
100ml (3½ fl oz) light soy
50ml (1¾ fl oz) dark soy
100g (3½oz) yellow rock sugar*
2 pieces dried mandarin peel
2 pieces cassia bark
4 star anise
1 knob ginger, sliced
4 garlic cloves, sliced
3 spring onions

"For the past six months he had been skimming spirits, wines, plates, cutlery and glassware, frypans, 20-litre tins of oil, CDs and so on. The guy had hoarded enough of my goods to start his own restaurant!"

A Cinderella Story

Blake's

Not long before the Christmas of 1991 I was approached by a vivacious redhead by the name of Barbie Ross. Barbie worked for the owners of Southgate, a new complex being built on the south bank of the Yarra River.

I was flattered to be approached by Southgate and well aware that I wasn't the first person to be offered a lease. In fact, I may have been the hundred and first person offered a lease. It didn't matter because only one of the previous parties was signed up. The recession was still having a profound impact on the restaurant industry, and as a result no-one would dare consider investing in new food ventures. For me, however, the approach was timely because I was considering what to do next. Christmas put a hold on negotiations and, as I wasn't in any position to put a restaurant together, I let it pass without another thought. But Barbie persisted after Christmas and I went along with it to see what might happen.

I made a presentation to the Southgate owners, with a design, menus, mock table settings and a swatch board of finishes, materials and colours. They liked my proposal enough to ask me to the next stage, which was to make a $2000 payment to get a look at the lease.

The deadline passed and I received a phone call very early the next morning asking me if there was a problem. There was no problem—unless you consider not having any money a problem. I told them about my predicament and apologised for wasting their time. They came back to me asking how much it would cost to fit-out according to the design. We guesstimated around $500,000, and to my surprise they said they would put $500,000 towards the fit-out of the space I was looking at. I was introduced to young gun architect Peter Maddison, who provided a new design that allowed me to buy every last piece of equipment, right down to vegetable peelers and wooden spoons. This was an absolute Cinderella story.

Jennie and I broke up three months before Blake's was due to open and I moved into a warehouse that a friend of mine owned. When I say warehouse, I mean the industrial, concrete floors, no heating, unglamorous type. I slept on a mattress on the floor and borrowed my mother's car for a month to get around.

The fit-out went according to plan and the closer the restaurant got to completion, the more amazed I was at how I got into this position. I was regularly shaking my head in disbelief or pinching myself to see if I would wake up from some fantastic dream.

Southgate was declared open on Friday 4th of September 1992, with a party for 5000 invited guests. Most restaurants managed to get operational for the opening, if only just. Our tradesmen handed over the tenancy to us at 1pm, just five hours before we were due to open. Food and wine were delivered throughout the morning. To get open I had to write cheques worth $8000—and I had no money in the bank. First thing Monday morning I banked $12,000 from the weekend's takings to cover the cheques and we were up and running.

Grant Van Every was a champion sommelier and a great mate from my time in Sydney. We talked about him coming down to Melbourne to be my sommelier at Blake's and he jumped at the chance, mainly because he would be closer to the mecca of golf: Melbourne's Sandbelt and Mornington Peninsula golf courses. He came up with the idea of having a suggested wine by the glass with every dish on our menu, which really gave us a great point of difference from other restaurants. It was an instant hit, but with a fair amount of wastage during quieter times it proved to be costly for me. You will be happy to know that any wines that weren't considered servable were consumed by the staff at the completion of their shift and not poured down the sink!

My knowledge of wine is not vast, but everything I do know I learnt from Grant. He also passed on his knowledge to any floor and kitchen staff willing to listen. Grant held a wine education session for the staff on a weekly basis, and it served as an opportunity to check out wine samples that had been left by reps seeking inclusion on our list. All bottles were masked so there could be no playing favourites with an acknowledged great wine. One day we might have had 15 or so Chardonnays to taste blind and the following week may have been 18 Cabernets. Each week a different variety, and each week the wines were marked on a score sheet that was circulated to each participant. Scores were collated and the best wines decided by a democratic vote for placement on our list.

The kitchen featured three wood-burning cooking stations. We had a wood-fired oven, a wood-fired rotisserie and a wood-fired char grill. They all became a bit of a nightmare in their own way. The oven and rotisserie were linked to the same extraction system which had to travel up three floors and exit next to the old Sheraton Hotel directly above us. A strong motor had to be installed to draw the smoke up that length of flue, and as a result it sucked too much heat out of the oven. Baffles were installed so that the kitchen staff could regulate the airflow and it took a couple of months to get the balance right.

The char grill was even worse. Yes, the cooking results were fantastic, but because the fans weren't strong enough we had smoke exiting the open kitchen and escaping into the restaurant. The longer service went, the worse the smoke got and all complaints to centre management fell on deaf ears. Everything came to a head when I went out to talk to a couple of tables one night and noticed very fine ash had settled on the shoulders of guests sitting close to the kitchen.

Looking back now, the whole thing was comical, but at the time it was no laughing matter. It is difficult enough running a busy restaurant and trying to stay on top of your game without having to go through these issues. They were out of my hands and beyond my capabilities, yet I still had to suffer the consequences.

One morning not long after we opened we had a visit from Frank Van Handel, who at the time owned The Stokehouse with his brother John. I thought it was a social visit because my floor manager Damian and I had both worked for the Vans. I was very wrong.

Frank was angry and demanded to have a 'chat' with Damian and me. He lined us up against a wall and, with index finger pointed in a very threatening manner, proceeded to give both of us a severe dressing down. I hadn't been made to feel like that since getting the strap at state school. I had absolutely no idea why and the fact that I put up with it, I can only put down to being in a state of shock.

As it turned out, Damian, while having a long leisurely lunch, had been seen handing out Blake's Restaurant business cards in The Stokehouse dining room to regular Stokehouse patrons. If I was Frank I would have been furious as well, only I may have made a phone call first to clarify if I had any involvement. Either way, I was guilty by association only because I had no knowledge of Damian's actions and certainly would not have been party to it.

One day in our first year, I arrived and checked out the previous night's figures. It was a Monday night in the depths of winter and while we were relatively quiet, we were by no means as quiet as the cash register reconciliation suggested. So I locked myself in my six-foot-by-six-foot office with the cash register roll and manual for a bit of amateur forensic accounting. Very suspiciously, with only 40 patrons for the evening, 10 steaks had been voided at midnight after the last guest had left. I checked with the kitchen and only five or six steaks had been sold for the evening. I learnt that it was possible to void items after the issue of receipt.

Not being one to jump to conclusions, I spent the next two days going through six months' worth of cash register rolls. What I uncovered shocked and angered me to my core. There was a pattern of this 'voiding after issue of receipt' that coincided regularly with the evening before the suspect's two days off. I considered all possible explanations because I did not want to believe that this person could steal from me, but the evidence was damning. I was having a fair bit of money stolen by someone I trusted, someone I gave responsibility to and who was being well looked after.

Unfortunately this wasn't the only time I had to contend with theft. I employed a cleaner. I had been told that he was facing armed robbery charges but he was adamant that he was innocent. Being the type of person that can only see the good in everyone, I believed him and gave him a job. Over the next six months I lent him money for legal fees and even took him and his son to the football a couple of times. His idea of gratitude was to twice sledgehammer open a small safe in my office within three weeks for a combined haul of $14,000.

On investigation the police searched his apartment. In the ceiling space they found half my money, the other half having already been spent on, among other things, a bike and leather jacket. It was a relief to get my money back and I had insurance for the balance that had been spent.

But the police found more. For the past six months he had been skimming spirits, wines, plates, cutlery and glassware, fry pans, 20-litre tins of oil, CDs and so on. The guy had hoarded enough of my goods to start his own restaurant! He was found guilty of armed robbery and got a couple of years in jail.

In 1993, my partner Mischee and I were invited to attend Oaks Day at the Spring Racing Carnival as guests of Con Andronis, owner of Clamms, our seafood supplier. I had just gotten over the thefts and thought a nice relaxing time at one of Australia's premier days of racing would be good therapy.

new years eve 1999

a small bombay sapphire martini

lobster & truffle arancini
oyster & pidgeon wonton
smoked salmon stackette

emilio lustau extra-fino sherry

*****

moreton bay bug & pomelo salad with vietnamese mint & chilli
or
steamed coral trout on a sauté of asparagus & asian greens with soy butter

1983 josmeyer riesling 'hengst' 'cuvee de la st martin' grand cru
&
1988 leo buring 'leonay' riesling

*****

pheasant sausage with champagne cabbage & beetroot glaze
or
saltwater duck breast with turnip cake & star-anise jus

1996 gevrey chambertin grand cru burgundy
&
1996 bass philip premium pinot noir

*****

'blakes' tournedos rossini- fillet steak on a truffle crouton with
whole lobe foie gras & victorian wild morel sauce
or
'blakes' veal cordon bleu- parmesan crumbed baby veal cutlet stuffed with prosciutto & tallegio on braised baby fennel

1997 chapoutier hermitage
&
1994 jasper hill 'emily's' paddock shiraz

*****

a selection of cheddars from around the world

1982 penfolds 'grange' hermitage

*****

baked sauternes custard with passionfruit sauce & wafer biscuit

1990 château de fargues sauternes
&
1990 de bortoli noble one

at midnight
1990 dom perignon
served in a commemorative 'riedel' champagne glass to take home
driven home in 'blakes' mini bus(within a radius of 8 km)

Cost $1000- per person

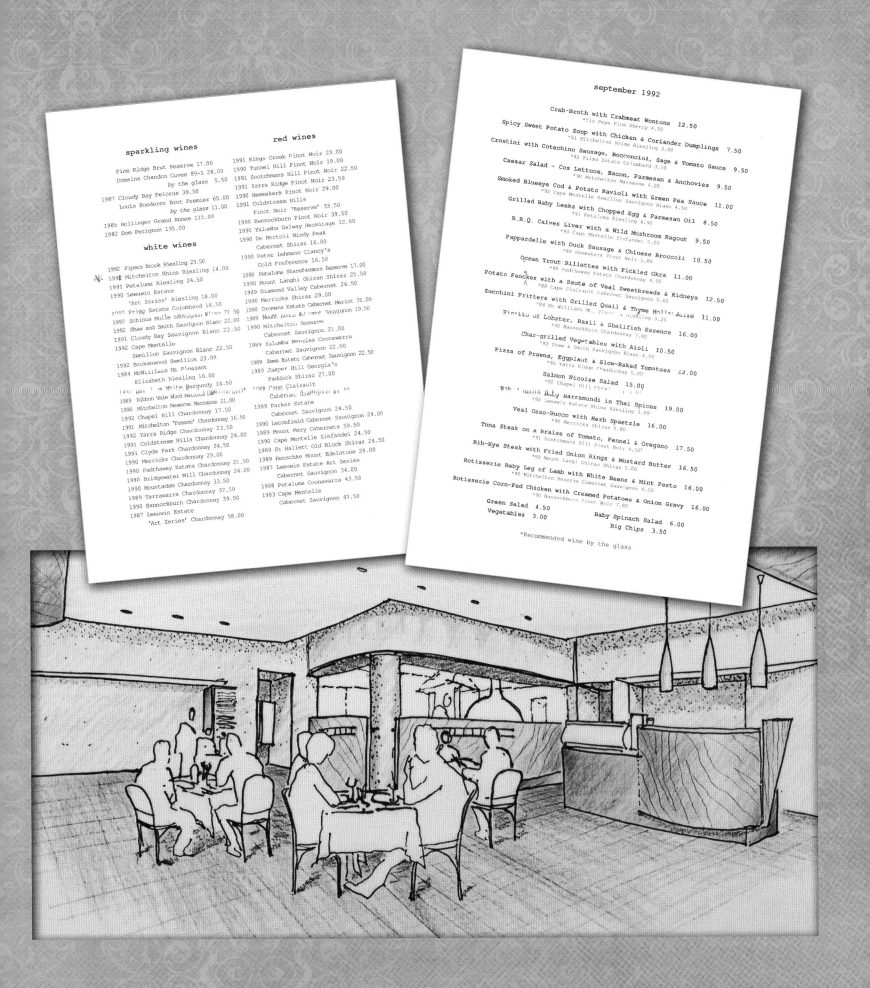

sparkling wines

Pine Ridge Brut Reserve 17.00
Domaine Chandon Cuvee 89-1 28.00
    by the glass 5.50
1987 Cloudy Bay Pelorus 39.50
Louis Roederer Brut Premier 65.00
    by the glass 11.00
1985 Bollinger Grand Annee 115.00
1982 Dom Perignon 195.00

white wines

1992 Pipers Brook Riesling 23.50
1991 Mitchelton Rhine Riesling 14.00
1991 Petaluma Riesling 24.50
1990 Leeuwin Estate
    'Art Series' Riesling 18.00
1992 Primo Estate Colombard 16.50
1992 Schinus Molle Sauvignon Blanc 21.50
1992 Shaw and Smith Sauvignon Blanc 22.00
1991 Cloudy Bay Sauvignon Blanc 22.50
1992 Cape Mentelle
    Semillon Sauvignon Blanc 22.50
1992 Brokenwood Semillon 23.00
1984 McWilliams Mt Pleasant
    Elizabeth Riesling 16.00
1991 Dom ? White Burgundy 14.50
1989 Ribbon Vale Wood Matured ...
1990 Mitchelton Reserve Marsanne 21.00
1992 Chapel Hill Chardonnay 17.50
1991 Mitchelton 'Preece' Chardonnay 16.50
1992 Yarra Ridge Chardonnay 23.50
1991 Coldstream Hills Chardonnay 24.00
1991 Clyde Park Chardonnay 24.50
1990 Merricks Chardonnay 29.00
1990 Padthaway Estate Chardonnay 21.50
1990 Bridgewater Mill Chardonnay 24.00
1990 Mountadam Chardonnay 33.50
1989 Tarrawarra Chardonnay 37.50
1990 Bannockburn Chardonnay 39.50
1987 Leeuwin Estate
    'Art Series' Chardonnay 58.00

red wines

1991 Kings Creek Pinot Noir 23.00
1990 Tunnel Hill Pinot Noir 19.00
1991 Scotchmans Hill Pinot Noir 22.50
1991 Yarra Ridge Pinot Noir 23.50
1990 Heemskerk Pinot Noir 29.00
1991 Coldstream Hills
    Pinot Noir 'Reserve' 33.50
1990 Bannockburn Pinot Noir 39.50
1990 Yalumba Galway Hermitage 12.00
1990 De Bortoli Windy Peak
    Cabernet Shiraz 16.00
1990 Peter Lehmann Clancy's
    Gold Preference 16.50
1990 Petaluma Sharefarmers Reserve 17.00
1990 Mount Langi Ghiran Shiraz 25.50
1989 Diamond Valley Cabernet 26.50
1990 Merricks Shiraz 29.00
1990 Dromana Estate Cabernet Merlot 31.00
1989 Mount Avoca ? Sauvignon 19.50
1990 Mitchelton Reserve
    Cabernet Sauvignon 21.00
1989 Yalumba Menzies Coonawarra
    Cabernet Sauvignon 22.00
1989 Zema Estate Cabernet Sauvignon 22.50
1989 Jasper Hill Georgia's
    Paddock Shiraz 27.00
1988 Cape Clairault
    Cabernet Sauvignon ?
1989 Parker Estate
    Cabernet Sauvignon 24.50
1990 Leconfield Cabernet Sauvignon 24.00
1989 Mount Mary Cabernets 59.50
1990 Cape Mentelle Zinfandel 24.50
1989 St Hallett Old Block Shiraz 24.50
1989 Henschke Mount Edelstone 28.00
1987 Leeuwin Estate Art Series
    Cabernet Sauvignon 34.00
1988 Petaluma Coonawarra 43.50
1983 Cape Mentelle
    Cabernet Sauvignon 47.50

---

september 1992

Crab-Broth with Crabmeat Wontons 12.50
Tio Pepe Fino Sherry 4.50
Spicy Sweet Potato Soup with Chicken & Coriander Dumplings 7.50
91 Mitchelton Rhine Riesling 3.00
Crostini with Cotechino Sausage, Bocconcini, Sage & Tomato Sauce 9.50
92 Primo Estate Colombard 3.50
Caesar Salad - Cos Lettuce, Bacon, Parmesan & Anchovies 9.50
90 Mitchelton Marsanne 4.20
Smoked Blueeye Cod & Potato Ravioli with Green Pea Sauce 11.00
92 Cape Mentelle Semillon Sauvignon Blanc 4.50
Grilled Baby Leeks with Chopped Egg & Parmesan Oil 8.50
91 Petaluma Riesling 4.90
B.B.Q. Calves Liver with a Wild Mushroom Ragout 9.50
90 Cape Mentelle Zinfandel 5.00
Pappardelle with Duck Sausage & Chinese Broccoli 10.50
90 Heemskerk Pinot Noir 5.80
Ocean Trout Rillettes with Pickled Okra 11.00
90 Padthaway Estate Chardonnay 4.50
Potato Pancakes with a Saute of Veal Sweetbreads & Kidneys 12.50
88 Cape Clairault Cabernet Sauvignon 5.60
Zucchini Fritters with Grilled Quail & Thyme Hollandaise 11.00
84 McWilliams Mt Pleasant Riesling 3.20
Risotto of Lobster, Basil & Shellfish Essence 16.00
90 Bannockburn Chardonnay 7.80
Char-grilled Vegetables with Aioli 10.50
92 Shaw & Smith Sauvignon Blanc 4.50
Pizza of Prawns, Eggplant & Slow-Baked Tomatoes 12.00
92 Yarra Ridge Chardonnay 5.00
Salmon Nicoise Salad 15.00
92 Chapel Hill Chard...
Baby Barramundi in Thai Spices 19.00
90 Leeuwin Estate Rhine Riesling 3.90
Veal Osso-Bucco with Herb Spaetzle 16.00
90 Merricks Shiraz 5.80
Tuna Steak on a Braise of Tomato, Fennel & Oregano 17.50
91 Scotchmans Hill Pinot Noir 4.50
Rib-Eye Steak with Fried Onion Rings & Mustard Butter 16.50
90 Mount Langi Ghiran Shiraz 5.00
Rotisserie Baby Leg of Lamb with White Beans & Mint Pesto 16.00
90 Mitchelton Reserve Cabernet Sauvignon 4.20
Rotisserie Corn-Fed Chicken with Creamed Potatoes & Onion Gravy 16.00
90 Bannockburn Pinot Noir 7.80

Green Salad 4.50
Vegetables 3.00
Baby Spinach Salad 6.00
Big Chips 3.50

*Recommended wine by the glass

We caught the train to Flemington and arrived just before the start of the first race. No sooner had I stepped off the train than an announcement came over the public address system: 'Andrew Blake, please go to the secretary's office immediately.'

I was hoping that there might have been more than one Andrew Blake at the races but no such luck. 'Please call your restaurant urgently' was the message. I called from their phone. No answer. This was unusual considering we were full for lunch and a dozen staff were on deck waiting for the first customers. I rang Walter's Wine Bar at the other end of Southgate to see if anything unusual was going on, only to be told that they couldn't see anything except for smoke and a couple of helicopters hovering overhead!

Mischee and I walked briskly to the taxi rank and asked to be taken to Southgate. The driver said that we should avoid Southgate because a restaurant had caught fire.

What happened after that was surreal. Everything seemed to be going in slow motion. I was in a hurry to get to Blake's to confirm that it was my restaurant that was burning, but the traffic was heavy. We got out of the cab in the city to walk across the footbridge to Southgate. We didn't run, we just walked, possibly because we didn't want to see what we knew had occurred.

As we arrived the fire crews were mopping up. A live wire in the ceiling cavity had come in contact with an air conditioning duct and fire quickly spread through the ducting. Sprinklers went off in the ceiling cavity and extinguished the fire, but the weight of the water brought the ceiling crashing down. The restaurant was flooded and the water damage was great. Most of the furniture was destroyed and foods out ready for lunch were spoiled. Great sections of the spotted pine floor had to be ripped up, firstly to pump out water that had accumulated under the boards and then for industrial blow heaters to dry out the saturated wood. Electrical wires were hanging everywhere and lights had blown. The place was an absolute mess.

But 24 hours later we were open again ready for lunch service. How we did it was just an amazing story of cooperation between Southgate centre management, centre cleaners, tradesmen and my staff. The floorboards that were ripped up were temporarily replaced by chipboard sheets, with some gaps left to allow for continued drying. Plaster was reapplied to the hanging ceiling where great holes had appeared. Electricians rewired all that had been burnt out. Mischee and I spent the night on our hands and knees scraping up the sludge that had settled on the floor once the water had gone. The next morning 20 tradesmen worked feverishly to have the restaurant operational by midday and we did it. Bentwood chairs were borrowed from Thonet, new flowers were arranged, food was prepared—the whole place was ready to go, albeit appearing patched up and much the worse for wear. If I weren't in a complex like Southgate it would have taken weeks to reopen.

In 1994 I took on a partner in the business. Terry Christie was an old school mate from the 1970s but we had kept in close contact over the years, especially when we were both residing in Sydney. Terry knew nothing about hospitality but was a great administrator. He brought to Blake's a level of professionalism that had been lacking. I just wanted to have fun cooking and owning a busy restaurant but sometimes it felt like we were on board a runaway train. We were always busy: the money came in and went out without much control. I had always been too benevolent to make hard decisions that were in the best interests of the restaurant. Terry was the hard man that brought Blake's into line.

I cannot remember how Blake's Restaurant got involved with the first Australian Formula One Grand Prix in Melbourne. All I remember is working very hard to lose $5000. As a four-day event, we had to do some serious business in order to cover the $18,000 it cost us to set up a restaurant trackside. All requirements had to be hired through the Grand Prix Corporation, who added a 25 per cent margin to everything, and we were given enough room for 50 seats. Business was good but not good enough, so very early on the Sunday morning I moved my barricades out to encroach on the public space and slipped another 25 chairs in under the cover of darkness. Blake's at Southgate was very busy lunch and dinner, so all my prep for the Grand Prix restaurant had to be done once the last meals left the kitchen at around 11pm. By 3am or 4am the work was done, leaving enough time for two or three hours of sleep before making the day's deliveries to the track. My great friend and fellow chef Ian Curley came over on the Friday night after work and helped me cook through the night. Needless to say, I wasn't interested in doing subsequent Grand Prix.

There was one good thing that came out of the Grand Prix. I received two tickets from American Express to enjoy some corporate hospitality in their box at the end of the main straight. Mischee was heavily pregnant with our first child and I gave her a ticket saying I would be up in the box in 20 minutes. Jennie and Mischee were not that fond of each other in those days, so I gave the other ticket to Jennie, also saying that I would see her up in the box shortly. I had hoped that by being forced together they might bury the hatchet. I would love to have seen their faces as they saw each other instead of me. Anyway, my plan worked and they have been very close ever since, even buying a holiday house together at Aireys Inlet.

I was a guest chef for two weeks at The Excelsior hotel in Hong Kong in 1995. Most of the produce I had arranged was correctly certified for export and made it through Customs. Unfortunately the kangaroo fillets didn't arrive, so I rang Grant, who was departing Melbourne for Hong Kong the next day. In a last-ditch effort to get the roo to Hong Kong, I had Grant pack 20 kilograms of it in his luggage. It worked a treat. Grant and his luggage cleared Customs and we got back to my room at The Excelsior to unpack. We opened the suitcases to find the fillet bags had split and Grant's clothes were saturated with roo blood. Grant spent the next 24 hours in his hotel dressing gown waiting for his clean clothes to come back from the laundry.

On another guest chef trip I cooked at the Peninsula Beverly Hills for a week, commemorating the start of Qantas flying non-stop to LA. I arrived with my assistant Dean Hodgkinson to find our workload had increased dramatically. The Peninsula had been raided by Immigration the day before and they had lost 30 per cent of their staff, so we had to do all preparation ourselves for the special lunches and dinners.

In 1998, a certain Melbourne food critic was starting to get under my skin. I love my industry and don't like the people in it being savaged unnecessarily. Within a couple of weeks of starting his newspaper column he was telling Greg Malouf, who was at O'Connell's at the time, how to suck eggs and then giving The Flower Drum, one of Melbourne's leading restaurants for years, an abysmal failure. Part of the critic's modus operandi was to be controversial in order to make up for his poor wordsmithing and it generally involved trying to cut down tall poppies. I wrote a letter to his editor, which was published and created a bit of brouhaha. I received a call from the producers of a morning talk show asking me if I would appear with the critic.

The interview was hilarious. Someone from the show came into the green room before our appearance and tried to whip me into a frenzy. He reminded me of an ugly scene on live television a couple of years earlier where Normie Rowe went face to face with Ron Casey and punches were thrown. He suggested that I could take the same sort of action if I was angry enough.

Nothing much happened. Barbs were thrown, insults made and in the end it was a non-event. But I only had to wait a couple of weeks to see him get his comeuppance. On MediaWatch it was revealed that the critic had been a paid publicist for Crown Casino restaurants and that he had trouble seeing that there was a conflict of interest. If a glowing Crown-paid 'review' of Silks within weeks of a Flower Drum panning didn't qualify as a major conflict of interest then I don't know what would.

In September 1998, a huge explosion at the Esso Natural Gas Plant in Gippsland affected gas supplies to Melbourne for three weeks. Many restaurants were forced to close their doors but because we had both a wood-burning char grill and wood-fired oven, all I had to do was buy a couple of bottled gas burners for pan work and we were still operational. We put together a slightly condensed menu and Blake's stayed open. Many other restaurants had to close until the gas supply resumed, and so business for us was huge.

Not long into 1999 I started planning for New Year's Eve. The changing of millenniums could not go by without a bit of a bash, especially as I had almost killed myself in a car accident in May. Blake's was in the dress circle for a spectacular fireworks display on the Yarra and I wanted to do something that would set a high mark.

I set a price of $1000 per person for dinner and then worked backwards, putting together something special that would give my guests value for money, even at that heady price. The menu was true to our style and I didn't once feel tempted to go over the top with the dishes, following our credo that superior ingredients always speak for themselves. I wanted to offer two wines with each course: one a Grand Cru from France and the other an iconic Australian wine that would try to give the import a run for its money. I contacted Gary Steele, a great friend of mine and owner of Domaine Wine Shippers. With French wines from Gary's formidable stable and the Australian wines I had in storage, we came up with an amazing line-up.

The night was truly memorable, from the small martini on arrival to the magnums of 1990 Dom Perignon poured at midnight while guests watched fireworks on the terrace. But that was not the end of our work. The idea of abandoning my guests to a mile-long taxi queue was just not on, so we hired two minibuses and shuttled everyone home to their door between 1am and 3am. I went to bed feeling very satisfied that I had not only delivered the goods, but exceeded everyone's expectations as well.

Blake's doors closed for the last time on August 11, 2002. I had mistakenly taken a lease on a tenancy to expand and create Blake's Backdoor, another one-stop providore operation. But I lost interest once an opportunity in Greville Street came my way and decided not to proceed. Unfortunately I could not get out of the lease. My combined rents were more than a thousand dollars a day and I fell behind in my payments during the winter when cash flow dropped right away.

Blake's as a restaurant was dead. I had used it as a cash cow to help shore up other failing businesses and I finally bled it dry. I regret many things I have done, and one of the worst was not showing my restaurant the respect it deserved. As a standalone restaurant it was wildly successful but it was burdened by my other poor decisions. It was the flagship that established me as a chef of standing and afforded me a great lifestyle. And like most who get caught up in such self-indulgence, the crash was inevitable.

My life revolved around Blake's and now my security blanket was gone. While Jennie and Mischee arranged for the physical dismantling of Blake's, I went away to far north Queensland for four days to ponder my immediate future.

"[Blake's] was the flagship that established me as a chef of standing and afforded me a great lifestyle."

Blake's Restaurant

Team at Blake's (1993)

roast rack of lamb, eggplant, anchovy and buffalo mozzarella moussaka

Cut eggplant into 7mm (¼in) thick slices. They should all be of a uniform diameter of around 6cm (2⅜in). Pan-fry the slices in olive oil so that they are cooked and lightly browned on both sides. Put aside.

Cut buffalo mozzarella into thin slices and put aside.

Cut anchovy fillets in half lengthways and put aside.

Lay 16 eggplant slices out on a baking tray. Spoon a little reduced tomato sugo on each, then top with a sliver of anchovy, then a basil leaf and finish with a slice of buffalo mozzarella. Stack these slices on top of each other to create four stacks with four layers on each. Grind a little black pepper on each and put aside.

In a heavy pan over high heat, seal lamb racks on all surfaces. Place in an oven at 160°C (325°F) for around 12 minutes until medium rare, then rest in a warm place.

Deglaze the pan that the lamb cooked in with Shiraz. When reduced by half, add the demi-glaze and simmer for one minute. Strain, add olives and reduce to a sauce consistency.

Heat eggplant moussaka gently in a medium (180°C, 350°F) oven until warmed through and the mozzarella melts.

Serve the lamb racks with a moussaka and olive jus.

3 small–medium sized eggplants
Olive oil
1 ball buffalo mozzarella
8 anchovy fillets
1 cup tomato sugo, reduced to hold its shape
16 basil leaves
Black pepper, to taste
4 x 5-rib racks of lamb
½ cup Shiraz
1 cup demi-glaze or reduced veal stock
½ cup Kalamata olives, pitted and cut into quarters

gremolata crumbed buffalo mozzarella with beet leaves, golden beets and hazelnuts

Juice large beetroot and reduce on the stove by around 80 per cent until it becomes a syrupy essence.

Cook baby beets, peel and halve.

Toast hazelnuts, peel and quarter roughly.

Mix breadcrumbs with lemon zest, minced garlic and chopped parsley.

Cut mozzarella rounds in half flatways to create two discs about 1cm (⅜in) thick. Dust lightly with flour, dip in eggwash and then in crumb mixture.

In a large frypan, heat extra virgin olive oil and butter until butter starts to foam. Add crumbed mozzarellas and cook until golden brown. Flip and repeat other side.

Wet beet leaves with a little extra virgin olive oil and red wine vinegar. Season with sea salt and cracked black pepper.

Divide leaves between four plates and add the baby golden beets and hazelnuts. Drizzle around a little hazelnut oil and red beet reduction. Place a molten disc of crumbed mozzarella on each salad and serve.

1 large red beetroot
1 bunch golden baby beets
½ cup hazelnuts
2 cups fresh course breadcrumbs
Grated zest of 1 lemon
1 garlic clove minced
2 tablespoon chopped parsley
2 x 125g (4oz) imported buffalo mozzarella
Plain flour
Eggwash
Extra virgin olive oil
30g (1oz) unsalted butter
Red wine vinegar
Sea salt and black pepper, to taste
2 handfuls baby beet leaves
Hazelnut oil

rice noodle cannelloni of asparagus and blueswimmer crabmeat with ginger-soy butter and coriander-peanut pesto

Mix coriander, lime zest, peanuts, ginger, red onion and peanut oil in a small bowl and season to taste.

Lightly peel and trim asparagus spears. Blanch in lightly salted water until cooked but still crisp to the bite. Refresh in iced water and drain.

Unroll a rice noodle roll and place the rectangle with the short side towards you. Place three asparagus spears along the front edge of the rice noodle sheet and scatter a quarter of the picked crabmeat and a quarter of the coriander leaves on the sheet. The asparagus tips should protrude by about 2cm (¾in). Season with sea salt and ground Szechwan pepper. Gently roll up the rice noodle sheet to form a 'cannelloni', with the asparagus in the centre.

Repeat the process for the other three sheets. Steam for about four minutes until hot.

While cannelloni are steaming, put ginger juice and gratings with the soy sauce in a non-corrosive saucepan. Bring to the boil and simmer until reduced by half.

Remove from heat and whisk in cold unsalted butter a little at a time. If need be, return saucepan to the heat and gently increase the temperature. When hot, but not boiling, remove from heat and incorporate remaining butter by whisking in a little at a time. Strain.

Spoon the ginger-soy butter over each of the cannelloni and garnish with sprigs of coriander.

1 bunch coriander, washed, picked and chopped
Zest of 1 lime
100g (3½oz) unsalted peanuts, roasted and chopped
1 teaspoon grated ginger
½ small red onion, minced
50ml (1¾ fl oz) fragrant peanut oil
12 asparagus spears
4 x 12cm (4¾in) rolls of fresh rice noodles
160g (5½oz) cooked fresh blueswimmer crabmeat
½ cup picked coriander leaves
Sea salt and Szechwan pepper, to taste
1 knob of ginger, finely grated and juices kept
40ml (1½ fl oz) light salt soy sauce
150g (5oz) unsalted butter
Coriander, to garnish

barbeque king prawns with a warm salad of baby artichokes and white beans with rosemary oil

Clean rosemary off the woody stems and put into a mortar and pestle with sea salt. Pound well until incorporated.

Put spice mix into a bar blender with olive oil and run motor for 30 seconds to mix well. Let infuse for 24 hours, shaking every couple of hours. Strain before using.

Trim artichokes of tough outer leaves. Cut off stem about 2cm (¾in) below the flower's base. Cut the top centimetre or so to remove tough tips.

Simmer in lightly salted water until tender all the way through. To test, insert the tip of a small sharp knife.

When cooked, refresh the artichokes in ice water. Drain and cut into quarters lengthways. Trim any other tough bits if necessary. Put aside.

Drain white beans and put into a saucepan. Cover with fresh cold water and bring to the boil. Simmer until just cooked enough that a bean will squash when pressed between your tongue and the roof of your mouth. Refresh, drain and put aside.

Scorch capsicums over a flame and cover with a cloth. When cool, peel off the charred skin and cut into 1cm (⅜in) squares.

Pit olives and cut into quarters.

In a bowl, place the white beans, artichoke quarters, red capsicum, olives and chopped parsley. Add the rosemary oil and red wine vinegar. Season with freshly ground black pepper and toss. Spread on a small platter.

Barbeque the prawns lightly and place on the artichoke bean mixture.

1 bunch rosemary
1 tablespoon sea salt
1 cup extra virgin olive oil
6 young globe artichokes
2 cups cannellini beans, soaked overnight
2 red capsicums
¾ cup Kalamata olives
3 tablespoons chopped flat-leaf parsley
½ cup red wine vinegar
Black pepper, to taste
12 large king prawns

rabbit lasagne with tomato, sage and truffle-scented béchamel

Heat olive oil in a heavy pan. Add rabbit legs and brown both sides. Transfer the legs to a roasting tray.

Add sliced onion and garlic to the heavy pan and sweat for two minutes. Add white wine, chopped tomatoes, thyme and bay leaves. Bring to the boil and pour over the rabbit legs.

Add veal stock, cover with foil and cook in an oven at 200°C (400°F) for 40 minutes or until the rabbit is tender.

Remove the rabbit legs from the braising liquid and cool.

Discard the thyme stalks and bay leaves from the braising liquid, add tomato paste and reduce until sauce thickens. Remove from heat and add olives, sage and parsley.

Strip rabbit meat from the bone and add to the sauce. Season with ground black pepper and sea salt to taste.

Bring milk to the boil and remove from heat.

In a saucepan, melt butter and stir in flour over a low heat to form a roux. Add milk a little at a time to the roux, stirring constantly. Once all the milk has been added stir in the provolone. Cook for two minutes over a low heat. Add truffle oil, season and cool.

Cut cooked lasagna sheets to fit four individual serve baking dishes.

Spoon a thin layer of rabbit mixture into each dish. Lay a cut lasagna sheet over this and spoon over béchamel. Repeat the process twice so that there are three layers each of the rabbit, pasta sheets and béchamel.

Sprinkle with a little grated provolone and bake at 180°C (350°F) for 15 minutes. Add a few drops of truffle oil just before serving.

4 tablespoons olive oil
8 rabbit legs
2 onions, sliced
4 garlic cloves, sliced
100ml (3½ fl oz) white wine
6 Roma tomatoes, peeled, seeded and chopped
¼ bunch thyme
3 bay leaves
1L (32 fl oz) veal stock
80g (2⅘oz) tomato paste
50g (1¾oz) Kalamata olives, pitted and quartered
1 tablespoon chopped sage
1 tablespoon chopped parsley
Black pepper and sea salt, to taste
400ml (13 fl oz) milk
50g (1¾oz) butter
50g (1¾oz) flour
½ cup provolone, grated
1 teaspoon truffle oil
12 cooked lasagna sheets
Extra provolone, grated

smoked salmon stack, pickled cucumber, horseradish cream and lattice chips

Peel potato and slice on a mandoline with the crinkle-cut blade. Turn the potato 90 degrees between each slice. Adjust the thickness if necessary so that each slice is perforated or 'latticed'.

Heat oil in a saucepan and fry the lattice-cut potatoes a couple at a time until golden brown and crispy.

Combine crème fraiche and horseradish in a bowl and mix, seasoning with a little freshly ground black pepper and sea salt.

Peel cucumber and take off long thin ribbons with a vegetable peeler or electric slicer. Salt the cucumber ribbons well and place in a sieve to drain off liquid for 15 minutes.

Rinse the salt off well and pat dry with absorbent paper. Place the wilted cucumber in a bowl with vinegar and sugar. Refrigerate.

To put together, place a lattice crisp in the centre of each plate. Then place in order: a layer of rocket, one and a half slices of smoked salmon, some ribbons of pickled cucumber, a dob of horseradish cream and another lattice crisp. Repeat sequence, finishing with a lattice crisp.

1 large potato
500ml (16 fl oz) vegetable oil
150ml (5¼ fl oz) crème fraiche
2 tablespoons freshly grated horseradish
Black pepper and sea salt, to taste
½ continental cucumber
2 tablespoons salt
50ml (1¾ fl oz) white wine vinegar
1 teaspoon caster sugar
40g (1½oz) rocket
12 slices premium smoked salmon

grilled cotechino sausage with warm potato salad and mustard fruits

Put seed mustard, vinegar and oil in a small jar. Screw on lid and shake vigorously to emulsify.

Simmer kipfler potatoes in lightly salted water until tender. While hot, peel and cut on a slight angle 8mm (5/16in) thick.

Place in a bowl with chopped chives and enough dressing to coat. Season with sea salt and freshly ground black pepper and toss very gently.

Cut Cotechino sausage into 1cm (3/8in) thick slices. Pan-fry slices in a little olive oil over a medium heat for one minute each side.

Share potatoes between four plates and drizzle with some excess dressing. Place overlapping slices of Cotechino sausage on each pile of potatoes. Top with diced mustard fruits and drizzle a little hot demi-glaze around each plate.

2 teaspoons seed mustard
30ml (1⅓ fl oz) white wine vinegar
120ml (4½ fl oz) extra virgin olive oil
300g (10oz) kipfler potatoes
1 cooked Cotechino sausage of about 600g (1lb 3½oz)
2 tablespoons chopped chives
Sea salt and black pepper, to taste
100g (3½oz) mustard fruits, cut into 5mm (¼in) dice
100ml (3½ fl oz) veal demi-glaze

seared sea scallop tart with babagannouj and basil oil

Holding the stems, immerse the whole bunch of basil into boiling water for five seconds and then refresh in ice water. Pat dry and blend in a bar blender with two cups of extra virgin olive oil.

Transfer to a large jar and let flavours infuse for 24 hours, shaking vigorously every few hours. Strain through a fine sieve lined with muslin cloth.

Using a 12cm (4¾in) pastry cutter, cut four discs out of two butter puff pastry sheets. Prick each pastry disc with a fork about 10 times to reduce the pastries' rising capacity.

Brush each disc with eggwash and bake at 200°C (400°F) for five minutes. Turn down to 180°C (350°F) and continue cooking for a couple of minutes until the pastry discs are golden brown.

Scorch eggplants over a naked flame on all sides and cool.

Cut eggplants open, scoop the flesh into a colander and drain for 10 minutes to eliminate any bitter flavours. Place eggplant flesh in a medium bowl, add remaining ingredients (except for scallops) and mash together.

Spread a generous amount of babagannouj on each pastry disc and warm in a low oven while preparing the scallops.

In a very hot frying pan wet with a little oil, sear the sea scallops for 30 seconds each side. Place four on each pastry disc and drizzle with basil oil.

1 bunch basil
2 cups extra virgin olive oil
2 pre-rolled butter puff pastry sheets
Eggwash
2 large eggplants
2 cloves garlic
¼–½ cup lemon juice (depending on taste)
6 tablespoons tahini
1 teaspoon salt
6 teaspoons olive oil
4 tablespoons yoghurt
16 large sea scallops

chicken and coconut salad with smoked quail eggs, chilli, peanuts and asian herbs

Bring master stock to a simmer and submerge chicken whole. Return to a simmer and cook for 20 minutes.

Remove the pot from the heat, leaving the chicken in the master stock as it cools.

Simmer quail eggs in water for two minutes and refresh in cold water. Carefully peel by rolling the quail egg on a bench with a little pressure to crack the shell.

Wet tea leaves with a little water and place in a wok. Put the peeled quail eggs on a round cake rack in the wok and place over a medium heat. When the tea leaves start to smoke, place an air-tight lid over the wok and smoke for two minutes. Put aside.

Reduce coconut milk, sugar and fish sauce by one-third. Cool and add vinegar and lime juice.

In a large bowl, mix together shaved coconut, bean shoots, red shallot, chilli, coriander, Thai basil, Vietnamese mint, peanuts and fried shallots.

Shred the chicken into small pieces and add to the bowl. Add enough dressing to bind the salad, but not drown it. Toss well to mix evenly but gently.

In the centre of each of four plates, place a square of banana leaf and top with salad mix. Top each salad with some threads of Kaffir lime leaf and place around halved quail eggs.

2L (64 fl oz) master stock (see recipe)
1 medium corn-fed free-range chicken
8 quail eggs
3 tablespoons tea leaves
425ml (14 fl oz) coconut milk
50g (1¾oz) palm sugar
45g (1½oz) fish sauce
2 tablespoons coconut vinegar
2 tablespoons lime juice
½ cup shaved coconut
½ cup bean shoots
1 red shallot, finely sliced
1 chilli, seeds removed and cut into rings
½ bunch coriander, picked
½ bunch Thai basil, picked
½ bunch Vietnamese mint, picked
2 tablespoons peanuts, roughly chopped
2 tablespoons fried shallots
Banana leaves for garnish
4 Kaffir lime leaves, cut into threads

sautéed duck livers with frisée, figs, cracklings and blackberry vinaigrette

Crush blackberries in a bowl with the back of a large slotted spoon. Add mustard, tarragon and sherry vinegar and whisk together. Add extra virgin olive oil in a slow steady stream while continually whisking. Season.

Cut duck skins into broad strips and shallow fry in olive oil until crispy. Transfer to absorbent kitchen paper.

Pat duck livers completely dry. On a very hot pan, sauté the livers in olive oil over a high flame. Do in two batches if necessary to maintain the heat. Remove the pan from the heat and allow livers to rest for two minutes.

Break the Frisee leaves from the base, wash and dry in a salad spinner. Put the leaves in a bowl and add enough blackberry vinaigrette to lightly coat. Divide between four plates and arrange the duck livers, figs and duck crackling in and around each salad so they all look balanced.

Finish with a small grind of black pepper.

½ cup blackberries
1 tablespoon Dijon mustard
1 tablespoon chopped tarragon
½ cup sherry vinegar
2 cups extra virgin olive oil
Skins of 4 duck breasts
400g (13oz) duck livers, trimmed of all connective sinews
40ml (1½ fl oz) olive oil
1 Frisee lettuce
4 figs, each cut into 6

barbeque leg of milk-fed lamb with tzatziki and a braise of baby fennel, tomato and olives

Mix yoghurt, grated cucumber, garlic, dried mint and chopped basil together in a bowl. Season and put aside.

Have your butcher bone the lamb leg out so that the meat is in one big flat piece. Marinate the lamb in three quarters of the cup of olive oil, lemon zest and rosemary for two hours at room temperature.

Heat remaining oil in a saucepan. Add onion and fennel and cook over a medium heat for five minutes to soften.

Add chopped tomatoes, veal stock and oregano. Cover saucepan with a lid and continue to cook over a low heat for 15 minutes.

Add Kalamata olives, stir, adjust seasoning to taste and remove from heat.

Drain the lamb of the oil, and pat dry with paper towelling. Season with sea salt and freshly cracked black pepper and place skin side down on a hot barbeque. Because baby lamb is very lean, very little flaring will occur. Cook for five minutes and then turn the lamb over and cook the other side for a further five minutes.

Place on a cake rack on a roasting tray and roast for 10 minutes at 190°C (375°F). Remove from the oven and rest for 20 minutes. Lamb should be pink right through. Return to the oven at 120°C (250°F) for five minutes.

Pour any juices that have drained from the lamb into the tomato–fennel mixture. Spoon the mixture onto serving plates. Top with sliced lamb leg and a generous dollop of tzatziki.

tzatziki
250ml (8 fl oz) Greek-style yoghurt
½ Lebanese cucumber, de-seeded and grated
1 small clove garlic, crushed
1 teaspoon dried mint
3 tablespoons chopped basil

Finely grated zest of 1 lemon
1 cup extra virgin olive oil
1 milk-fed lamb leg, de-boned
½ cup rosemary sprigs
1 medium onion, sliced
2 fennel bulbs, finely sliced
4 tomatoes, seeded and roughly chopped
2 cups veal stock
2 tablespoons picked oregano leaves
½ cup Kalamata olives, pitted and halved
Sea salt and black pepper, to taste

chermoula roasted kangaroo fillet, giant couscous, silverbeet and tahini yoghurt

Put all chermoula ingredients in a food processor and blitz until garlic and chillies have been ground to a paste.

Combine all tahini yoghurt ingredients in a bowl and mix well. Refrigerate until needed.

Dry kangaroo fillets with paper towelling to absorb any excess blood. Remove any sinew with a sharp boning knife.

Smear the kangaroo fillets with chermoula paste and let sit at room temperature for 20 minutes.

Heat a large heavy-based skillet and add a little olive oil. Seal the roo fillets well on all sides and roast in an oven at 180°C (350°F) for five minutes. Remove meat to a resting rack and keep warm.

Deglaze the roo pan with Shiraz and reduce by half. Add brown veal stock and reduce by a further half. Add couscous, silverbeet, tomato, onion and coriander and simmer gently for five minutes.

Portion the couscous mixture between four bowls. Cut each roo fillet in half on a sharp angle and drape over the couscous. Top with a dollop of tahini yoghurt.

chermoula
45g (1½oz) cumin seeds, roasted and crushed
15g (½oz) coriander seeds, roasted and crushed
25g (⅘oz) sweet paprika
15g (½oz) ground ginger
2 cloves garlic, roughly chopped
2 whole bullet chillies, roughly chopped, deseeded and scraped
2 whole lemons, juiced
100ml (3½ fl oz) olive oil
5g (⅕oz) white pepper
5g (⅕oz) salt

tahini yoghurt
120g (4oz) yoghurt
60g (2oz) tahini
1 tablespoon lemon juice
½ teaspoon ground cumin
Salt

kangaroo fillets & couscous
4 kangaroo fillets of 200g (6½oz) each
½ cup Shiraz
½ cup brown veal stock
2 cups cooked Israeli couscous
1 cup silverbeet, cleaned, torn and blanched
2 tomatoes, seeds removed and roughly diced
1 onion, sliced and caramelised
½ bunch coriander, leaves picked

strawberry fritters, fig vincotto and sour cream ice-cream

Bring cream and milk to a boil.

Cream yolks and sugar in a bowl and slowly pour in scalded liquid, whisking as you do.

Cook out the custard over a double boiler until it coats the back of a wooden spoon.

Cool quickly over a bowl of ice and churn in an ice-cream machine. Freeze in an airtight container.

In a medium bowl, combine flours. Whisk in sparkling ale and soda water and mix to a smooth thin batter. Let stand for 10 minutes before whisking out any residual lumps.

Combine raspberries and sugar in a non-corrosive saucepan and bring to the boil. Puree and strain, add lemon juice and cool.

Using a syringe, inject fig vincotto into the centre of each strawberry, leaving the calyx attached.

Heat deep fryer to 175°C (350°F). Dust strawberries with plain flour and dip in batter. Deep fry until golden brown and remove with a slotted spoon onto paper towelling.

Serve with raspberry sauce and a scoop of sour cream ice-cream.

250ml (8 fl oz) sour cream
250ml (8 fl oz) milk
6 egg yolks
100g (3½oz) sugar
125g (4oz) self raising flour
30g (1oz) cornflour
150ml (5¼ fl oz) sparkling ale
150ml (5¼ fl oz) soda water
125g (4oz) raspberries
50g (1¾oz) sugar
1 teaspoon lemon juice
50ml (1¾ fl oz) fig vincotto
16 large, perfectly ripe strawberries, unhulled
1½L (48 fl oz) vegetable oil

"[Geoff's] crispy skin duck was our signature dish and acclaimed by one critic as 'the best duck dish from a non-Asian restaurant ever'."

Stella

	2.00 each
Stella Oyster Selection *freshly shucked from far & wide*	12.50
'92 Yalumba 'D' 9.00	
Jerusalem Artichoke Soup *yabbie tails & sautéed apple*	13.00
'94 Prentice Chenin Blanc 5.50	
Tuna Carpaccio *with herb flowers, extra virgin olive oil & grissini*	13.00
'95 Alta Sauvignon Blanc 6.00	
1/2 Shell Scallops *with citrus butter & fried artichokes*	13.00
'95 Salitage Unwooded Chardonnay 6.50	
Cold Roast Veal *with tuna mayo, stewed peppers & capers*	10.50
'95 Pipers Brook Ninth Island Chardonnay 7.00	
Tomato, Goats Cheese, Pesto & Parmesan Pizza	15.50/19.50
'93 Mountadam Riesling 6.50	
Grilled Bug Tails *chilli cucumber salad, son-in-law egg*	13.50
'95 Shaw and Smith Sauvignon Blanc 7.50	
Pigeon & Wild Mushroom Cake *with a star anise scented jus*	11.50/15.50
'93 Yalumba Bush Vines Grenache 5.50	
Flat Noodles *with shredded braised oxtail & red grapes*	13.00/17.00
'93 Veritas Bulls Blood 8.00	
Rabbit Risotto *wilted radicchio, caramelized shallots*	17.50
'94 T'Gallant Tribute Pinot Gris 8.00	
Roast Chicken Salad *pancetta, pinenuts & crunchy cavalinga croutons*	19.00
'93 Yering Station Chardonnay 6.00	
Crispy Skin Duck *with lup chong, bok choi & more chinese flavours*	18.50
'94 Tucks Ridge Pinot Noir 7.00	
Yellow Thai Curry of Butterfish *with green paw paw & coconut rice*	18.50
'95 Grosset Polish Hill Riesling 7.00	
Seared Salmon *basil risotto, capsicum essence*	18.50
'93 Bannockburn Chardonnay 12.00	
BBQ Lamb Loin *brussel sprout leaves & bacon sautéed in walnut oil*	19.50
'93 Clarendon Hills Merlot 9.50	
Peppered Porterhouse Steak *mash, buttermilk onion rings*	
'93 Seville Estate Shiraz 9.50	36.00

Stella Favorites

28gm of Sevruga caviar *waxy potatoes, creme fraiche*	12.50/16.50
'Louis Roederer Brut Premier 13.50	
Pumpkin Tortellini *mustard fruits, lemon butter*	19.00
'95 Brokenwood Semillon 6.50	
Red Duck Curry *with coconut rice*	
'93 Spring Vale Pinot Noir 9.50	

		Green Salad 3.50
	5.00	**Raddichio Pear & Parmesan Salad** 6.50
Vegetables	5.00	**Caesar Salad** 8.50
Stir-Fried Chinese Greens	4.00	
Fat or Skinny Chips		9.50
Bittersweet Chocolate Souffle *jaffa ice-cream*		9.50
'Sabra Liqueur 5.80		
Butterscotch Semifreddo *peanut brittle*		9.50

Stella

	32.00
28gm of Sevruga caviar *pink-rye chats, creme fraiche*	
'85 Dom Perignon 29.00	
Tasmanian Pacific Oysters *shucked to order, chilli-lime dressing, crispy fried, spicy ginger sauce*	
'94 Coldstream Hills Fume Blanc 6.60	
Blue Swimmer Crab Broth *coriander, stir-fried bean shoots*	
'93 Solana White (Spain) 4.00	
Seared Beef Carpaccio *rocket leaves, aioli, parmesan*	
'93 Colonnade Pinot Noir 4.00	
Grilled Asparagus *chopped egg, truffle oil*	
'92 Sauvignon Grassa et Fils 7.00	
Smoked Salmon *rosti potato, lime cream*	
'94 Oakridge Chardonnay 5.00	
Potted Tongue & Cheek *red pepper relish, melba*	
'91 Dessilani Spanna 4.60	
BBQ King Prawns *white bean salad, rosemary*	
'91 Shaw and Smith Reserve Chardonnay	
Vine Ripened Tomato Pizza *pesto, cara...*	
'93 Castle Rock Pinot Noir 6.60	
BBQ Calamari Pizza *roasted peppers,*	
'93 Pemrortham Clare Valley Rhi...	
Pumpkin Tortellini *mustard frui...*	
'94 Petaluma Riesling 6.60	
Linguini *goats cheese, lemon & leek*	
'94 Alta Sauvignon Blanc 5.00	
Smoked Pigeon Risotto *grilled red onion, rainbow chard*	17.00
'93 Springvale Pinot Noir 8.60	
Grilled Chicken Breast *couscous, Moroccan spiced butter, pomegranate*	
'92 Givry 1er Cru (Clos de la Servoisine - Domaine-Joblot) 14.00	
Red Duck Curry *coconut rice*	18.50
'Stella Artois 4.50	
Cold Roast Salmon *baby beets, pink grapefruit, citrus oil*	
'91 Leeuwin Estate Art Series Chardonnay 14.00	18.50
Steamed Wild Barramundi *asparagus risotto, capsicum essence*	
'94 Yarra Ridge Chardonnay 6.60	15.00
Wild Boar Sausages *smokey baked beans*	
'87 Cornas Noel Verset 9.50	17.00
Lamb Cutlets *grilled vegetables, basil oil*	16.50
'90 Seville Estate Cabernet Sauvignon 7.00	
Steak Diane *french fried potatoes*	7.50
'92 Craiglee Shiraz 7.60	

	4.00	**Caesar Salad**	7.50
Vegetables	5.00	**Rocket & Parmesan Salad**	5.00
Stir-Fried Chinese Greens	3.50	**Fat or Skinny Chips**	3.50
Green Salad			9.00
Mango Souffle *mango sorbet*			8.00
'94 Yarra Ridge Botrytis Semillon 12.00			
Peanut & Butterscotch Semifreddo *peanut brittle*			7.00
'92 Muscat de Beaumes de Venise Durban 12.00			
Pineapple Fritters *licorice ice-cream*			7.50
'94 Mt Horrocks Cordon Cut Riesling 9.00			
Creme Brulee *summer berries*			7.00
'92 De Bortoli Noble One 13.00			
...anita, raspberry sauce			9.00

"You Know Nothing About Food!"

Stella & Stella @ Heide

Twice in my restaurant life I ended up taking over the lease of a favourite establishment. The first time was Tansy's. Tansy Good and her partner Marc Bouten had a very successful, critically acclaimed restaurant in Carlton which moved to Spring Street in the city in the early 90s. They spent a small fortune on a very smart fit-out, with a restaurant upstairs and bistro downstairs. But Tansy and Marc fell out, the business struggled and eventually closed in 1994.

Geoff Lindsay had left Stephanie's and took the position of chef at Blake's some months earlier. This was never going to be a long-term thing, more an opportunity for Geoff to get Stephanie's out of his system after four years of working there. Geoff and I had been talking about doing something together for some time, and one day he mentioned that there was a 'For Lease' board on the façade of Tansy's.

We arranged to have lunch at Blake's with the owner of Tansy's building. My restaurant was heaving while we lunched and discussed the idea of taking over the Tansy's space, which must have impressed the owner because we signed a lease on the Spring Street site a couple of weeks later. So Geoff, Grant Van Every and I were in business together.

We were at pains for a couple of weeks over what to call the new restaurant. It eventually came down to a conversation between friends about the Seinfeld episode that parodied A Streetcar Named Desire. 'Stella' was suggested and universally accepted.

Friends from King Enterprises developed coloured glass ashtrays and grissini holders with our signature 'S'. Our business cards had a series of short recipes on the reverse side in the hope that people would keep them and collect the set. The menu layout was inspired by those from Brasserie Lipp in Paris. We engaged the services of architect Peter Maddison again, this time for some very simple additions like banquette seating, wine racking and improved lighting. Grant Slaney's Modern Art Production Group created our logo and artwork, as they had done for Blake's.

Geoff was able to express himself through his food for the first time, just as I had been able to do at Arthur's. His crispy skin duck was our signature dish and acclaimed by one critic as 'the best duck dish from a non-Asian restaurant ever'. Our upstairs kitchen was converted into a duck 'hangar' and we had trouble keeping up with the demand. Grant put together a wonderful small wine list including wines by the glass and by the 30ml tasters. Together with great service and kitchen teams, we were awarded three chef's hats in *The Age Good Food Guide* in our first year of operation.

In 1997 we were approached by the Heide Museum of Modern Art with the idea of opening a second Stella on their premises. We sat down with the museum's solicitors to thrash out a lease agreement. At one point, one of their team suggested that the museum 'would have the power to veto any items on the menu'.

Grant said okay, provided we could veto any art they were intending to show. 'But you know nothing about art,' was the response.

'And you know nothing about food,' was Grant's retort!

Again through poor management, things fell down at Stella. We were top-heavy and the place really needed hands-on working partners, not managing partners. Stella was a small business being run as if it were a big business and I am sure Geoff and Grant would look back now and agree. We were all to blame, but as the senior partner, I should have been stronger and taken a firmer grip on the business. Some hard decisions had to be made and instead of making them, I let them slide. It is very hard to tell your partners that things need to change when they are also your friends. The longer we put off those hard decisions, the deeper Stella became bogged in debt.

Andrew Gunn and his wife Rosie were regular clients at Stella. They became good friends and it seemed a good time to sell my share when Geoff and Andrew announced that they would be going into business together. After all, Stella was the vehicle for Geoff's food, and I wasn't interested in relaunching the restaurant in another guise. We struck a financial agreement but I still ended up with a substantial debt, which again was serviced by Blake's.

Pearl, Andrew and Geoff's restaurant, was born in the following year and has been in Melbourne's top half dozen ever since. I am still a regular for his duck curry, without a doubt the best I have had anywhere.

whole deep-fried baby snapper with three-flavoured sauce and root crisps

Place tamarind in a small bowl. Add ½ cup water and let stand for 10 minutes. Knead tamarind in water to soften and pass through a small sieve, discarding solids. Measure ¼ cup liquid and set aside.

Add to a mortar, one at a time, coriander root, salt, chopped fresh chillies, garlic and shallots, pounding each ingredient with a pestle until smooth before adding the next.

In a small saucepan, heat the oil over medium-high heat. Add the paste and fry until fragrant, about two minutes.

Stir in palm sugar and remaining ¼ cup water, simmer until thick. Add reserved tamarind water and fish sauce, and continue to simmer until reduced and slightly thickened. Remove from heat, cool and add cucumber and lime juice.

Peel and finely slice the sweet potato, beetroot, Chinese potato, taro root and lotus root using a mandoline or electric slicer. Wash, pat dry and deep fry until crisp.

Score the flesh of each fish through to the bone with four or five slashes per side. Separate flanks by positioning toothpicks in the cavities, forcing the sides apart and allowing the fish to be served 'standing up'.

Heat oil to 180°C (350°F) and immerse fish standing up in a frying basket. When cooked, remove the fish to drain completely on paper towels. Remove the toothpicks.

To serve, spoon the sauce onto the centre of each plate. Place a whole fried fish upright on top and garnish with root crisps and coriander sprigs.

¼ cup tamarind pulp
¾ cup warm water
2 tablespoons scraped and chopped coriander root
2 pinches coarse salt
3 long red chillies, seeded and roughly chopped
4 garlic cloves, finely diced
5 red shallots, finely diced
2 tablespoons vegetable oil
½ cup palm sugar
6 tablespoons fish sauce
½ cup finely diced cucumber
3 tablespoons lime juice
1 small sweet potato
1 beetroot
1 Chinese potato
1 taro root
1 lotus root
4 plate-size baby snapper or similar whole fish
Cottonseed or vegetable oil for deep frying
Coriander to garnish

geoff lindsay's crispy-skin duck with lup cheong, bak choy and more chinese flavours

Toast Sichuan peppercorns in a dry pan until they crackle. Add sea salt and grind to a fine powder with a mortar and pestle.

The ducks should have no cuts or holes in the skin and the heads should be intact.

Place a piece of ginger and a star anise in each of the two cavities. Carefully close each cavity with a poultry skewer. Place a butcher's hook through each duck neck.

Blanch both ducks by dunking in boiling water for five seconds and hang in an area with good air circulation. At Stella, we used a large electric fan to guarantee air movement. Leave for at least two hours to air-dry.

Combine vinegar, maltose, water, bicarb, ginger and remaining six star anise in a pot and simmer for 10 minutes. Cool and dip each duck thoroughly in this syrup, making sure the ducks are well coated and have a lacquered appearance. Hang the ducks to air-dry again for at least two hours.

Preheat the oven to 180°C (350°F). Roast the ducks on oven racks over a water bath for 60–75 minutes.

Heat a wok, add oil and ginger. Stir-fry bak choy and lup cheong with a little water.

In a separate saucepan, heat hoisin with chicken stock.

Place a pile of bak choy and lup cheong in the centre of each plate. Ladle some hot sauce over the vegetables.

Remove the legs and breasts from the ducks, being careful not to damage the skin. Cut each leg and breast in half and place on top of the vegetables. Garnish with spring onions that have been finely sliced on an angle. Place a small dish of Sichuan salt on each plate and serve.

100g (3½ozs) Sichuan peppercorns
20g (²/₃oz) sea salt
2 x 2.2kg (4lb 6½oz) ducks, heads on
2 small pieces ginger
8 star anise
600ml (19½ fl oz) rice wine vinegar
250g (8oz) maltose
300ml (10 fl oz) water
1 tablespoon bicarbonate soda
1 knob ginger
1 slice ginger
2 bunches bak choy
100g (3½oz) lup cheong, sliced on an angle
250ml (8 fl oz) hoisin sauce
125ml (4 fl oz) chicken stock
½ bunch spring onions
Sichuan salt

quail sausage roll with verjus sauce

Bone quails in one piece, as you would for a galantine.

In a heavy pan with a little olive oil, brown the quail carcasses with onion, carrot, celery and garlic. Add juniper berries and deglaze pan with verjus until reduced by half.

Add veal stock and simmer for 30 minutes until the liquid thickens to a sauce consistency. Strain through a fine mesh sieve, season and put aside.

In a food processor, pulse chicken a few times until a rough textured mince has been created. Add garlic, thyme and egg white and quickly mix until properly incorporated.

Remove from food processor to a bowl and fold in cream. Season with freshly ground black pepper and sea salt.

In the middle of a large sheet of plastic wrap, place one of the boned quails skin side down. Spoon some chicken mixture along the centre of the quail. Using the plastic wrap, roll the quail and its stuffing in a sausage-like shape. The quail should completely enclose the chicken stuffing and should be enclosed in about three layers of kitchen wrap.

Tie both ends of the plastic wrap and repeat the process for the remaining three quails.

Poach the quail sausages in a water bath that is barely simmering for 15 minutes. Make sure that the sausages are submerged because they have a tendency to float. Remove from the water and cool.

Cut each sheet of puff pastry in half. Unwrap the quail sausages and pat dry.

Place one quail sausage at the end of the pastry rectangle and roll it up so that the overlapping join is on the underside of the sausage roll. Trim any puff pastry that overhangs. Repeat the process for the other three sausages.

Brush the quail sausage rolls with eggwash and rest in the fridge for 30 minutes.

Preheat oven to 220°C (420°F) and bake for eight minutes, then reduce heat to 200°C (400°F) and bake for a further 10 minutes until pastry is golden brown.

Cut each quail sausage roll on an angle and serve in a small pool of hot verjus sauce.

4 quails
2 tablespoons olive oil
1 onion, diced
1 carrot, diced
1 celery stick, diced
1 garlic clove, diced
6 juniper berries
100ml (3½ fl oz) verjus
400ml (13 fl oz) veal stock
200g (6½oz) chicken fillets
1 garlic clove, minced
½ teaspoon thyme leaves
2 egg whites
50ml (1¾ fl oz) cream
Black pepper and sea salt, to taste
2 sheets ready-rolled butter puff pastry
Eggwash

"The place was a great
venue and I was
very proud of what
I had created."

The Perils of Partnerships

Tonic

Angelo Tsaptsalis was a guy I met in the days when people went to The Botanical Hotel in South Yarra to party. Angelo worked there for Chris and Harry in the mid-80s, then left and went into business for himself, buying the old Iguana Bar in Chapel Street and reopening it as Citrus. It was a bad name for an ordinary place that had no ambience at all. Bars are about people, and once you lose the people you can say goodnight.

In 1995, Citrus was dying a slow death and Angelo asked me if there was anything I thought we could do to save it. He had spent a lot of money on getting the bar but nothing on changing whatever the problem was in the first place. When a bar dies, you need to do more than change the name to give it a new lease on life. Somehow, probably while having a big night, I discussed Citrus with Blake Dowe, a fellow party animal and tiler who dreamed of owning a bar.

We went to Angelo and made him an offer too good to refuse. He had to relinquish 66 per cent of a business that had one foot in the grave anyway, and in return Blake Dowe and I would come in and create a world-class bar. Angelo didn't have to put any money in, just take his debt from Citrus so we could start with a clean slate.

The room itself was a great space—just a normal shop front, but the ceilings were very high and the room deep, so it gave the bar a real sense of volume.

Some years earlier, I had been to a bar in New York City called The Merc Bar where I rested my feet on a cowhide ottoman. I loved that ottoman and thought if I ever had the opportunity to do a banquette in cowhide I would. So for Tonic we went to a hide wholesaler and bought 140 cowhides for the upholstery of substantial banquettes that became the main feature of the bar. Another feature was a tropical fish tank in a wall void at the entrance where the Iguana Bar menu was once housed. A long orange padded thing we used to call the jellybean was slung from the ceiling to help absorb noise and house hidden speakers that were pointed at the ceiling for optimum sound quality. Small, intimate tables and artisan table lamps made by Mark Douglass created a cosy ambience.

Glenby was still living in Sydney but he had left the Four in Hand hotel and indicated that he would come back to Melbourne if the right job came up. I wanted Tonic to be more than just a bar, so we offered Glenby the head chef's job to guarantee that the food would be everything we wanted it to be. He came down for a look and never went back. The food he created was an absolutely perfect fit for what we wanted.

The bar went off and for a while it was the place to be. Everyone wanted to get in so we had to employ the Amazonian Michelle to 'man' the door and control the number of patrons. We felt having a girl on the door would curb aggressive behaviour from people trying to get in and it worked well. Day trade was slow because the place looked and felt more like a nightclub, but it didn't matter because we were so busy at night. The food side of the business then became a burden on the bar because people were drinking and not eating.

It didn't take long for things to go awry. We went to a business broker and got a good price because of our Chapel Street location. Debts were paid but we were left with a $100,000 shortfall due to previously unknown, unpaid debts. I was the only partner who had the means to pay and did so over a period of time.

Going into partnership on this occasion was perhaps the worst mistake I have ever made, but it was typical of my decision-making process at the time.

Events Warehouse

Remember back to 1995. Melbourne's CBD was at the beginning of its renaissance. It was three years before the opening of the Crown Casino complex, seven years before Federation Square and eight years before New Quay at Docklands.

Southgate was the original restaurant and café complex before these others opened up and diluted our dining numbers. From 1992–1996 Blake's Restaurant, like all others at Southgate, got swamped. We were constantly booked out with regular diners, but we were also regularly booked out for functions, both corporate and private. With the views from Southbank over the Yarra River to the city behind, it was a much sought-after location for special events. I didn't like putting a sign on our front door reading 'sorry, closed for a private function', but as anyone in the industry knows, functions are easy money compared with the bump and grind of â la carte dining. Private functions in restaurants are one of those things that owners don't really like but learn to live with.

Some time in 1995, Terry and I met with a fellow who had a function barge that cruised up and down the Yarra. He had a location for a food business, but when he started talking about a 'fisherman's basket' type restaurant with a bar made out of an old boat we went cold on the idea pretty quickly.

The location was South Wharf, which, at the time, was never going to work as a restaurant strip, but I saw a fantastic opportunity to create a function space. It had a northwest aspect with none of the shading problems you get on the north bank, it was relatively isolated so noise would never be an issue, and it had a huge amount of car parking. Like my restaurant, it was just outside the CBD but overlooked the city. South Wharf was a great central and accessible location but very private. It gave us an opportunity to create a space where we could take all our function business away from my restaurant, but still give our function clients restaurant standard food.

We bypassed a number of people and spoke with the developers directly. They had grand plans of a thriving restaurant strip similar to Southgate but we knew it would never happen. The site we were interested in was the oldest and perhaps the most dilapidated. There had been a major fire about 10 years previous, so the roof and walls were gone. All that was left were the giant wharf doors and iron trusses. The floor was buckled and pitted and had slumped by more than 18 inches in one corner.

The developer promised to rebuild the wharf to its former specifications, giving us a great blank canvas from which to create a unique venue. If it was returned to its former glory then it was the perfect space for my Events Warehouse, as it was to be known.

I now had a venue that could seat 300 people on the Yarra River only a few hundred metres from the city. I had huge dark blue velvet curtains installed on tracking that allowed us to change the size of the room to suit the event. Simple canned spots were used for lighting.

My budget for the Events Warehouse was blown out of the water and I was forced to take on a partner to get everything to an operable stage. Con Andronis from Clamms had been my seafood supplier, supporter and friend for about five years and was very keen to get involved. I needed his cash injection desperately. He held the whip hand so I had to accept his proviso that he would only get involved if he had a controlling interest.

As a chef I had some great ideas, but as a businessman I fell way short. Everything I did was done without careful forward planning. I presumed that everything would just fall into place and my cash flow from Blake's would fund projects like Events Warehouse. Now I had lost control of my pet project. Con moved his partner Dorothy in and all of a sudden I felt like an outsider, less than welcome in my own business.

We had some spectacular events in the time I was a partner. People in Melbourne knew the quality of my product and were generally ecstatic to be able to have such quality at a large function. Previously one would have to be content to be in the bowels of a five-star hotel to have such events, and then you had to contend with 'hotel food'. Now you could arrive by boat and step into our space through huge sliding glass doors that opened up onto broad decking overlooking the city.

Our first function was a large Jewish wedding. I first met with the families 10 months before their wedding—nine months, three weeks before my venue was ready! I took them to South Wharf to show them my site.

'The entrance and bar will be over here and the main room with river and city views will be here,' I said.

'The kitchen will be behind the bar and bathrooms to the right over there,' I added, fingers and arms flailing.

I invited the families to a tasting preview at my restaurant and they booked. They booked the biggest function of their lives based on a walk-through of a derelict site with a stranger that had a vision! And it was a fantastic day that they had too.

Another event I will always remember was the launch for a new women's fashion magazine that only managed to publish four monthly instalments before folding. We accepted a partial contra deal on advertising with the magazine, but we were still owed $25,000 for quite some time.

We eventually received payment, but even that had a bit of drama about it. A cheque was given to Con at home and the delivery guy was accompanied by four dark cars, strategically positioned outside. These guys had obviously watched too many gangster movies!

Con and I had plenty of heated arguments ourselves. It was impossible for two alpha males to be in partnership and we agreed to part ways. Con bought me out which was fine at the time, but every time I stepped back into Events Warehouse I actually regretted selling my share. The place was a great venue and I was very proud of what I had created.

Events Warehouse

"Our first function was a large Jewish wedding. I first met with the families 10 months before their wedding, nine months, three weeks before my venue was ready!"

snapper, mussel, leek and semillon pie

Sweat leek and garlic in butter in a heavy pan for one minute. Add flour and cook without colour for another minute.

In a saucepan, bring Semillon to the boil and add mussels. Cover and steam.

When mussels have opened, tip into a colander, reserving the cooking liquor. Add this liquid to the leek roux and stir in well.

Heat milk and add a little at a time, mixing well between each addition. A smooth, thick white sauce should result. Add grain mustard and dill and season with freshly cracked black pepper and sea salt.

When the sauce has cooled a bit, stir in snapper chunks and mussels. Refrigerate.

Lightly brush four deep individual pie moulds with butter. Line with puff pastry and trim. Fill each pastry-lined pie mould with the snapper mixture and cover with a pastry lid.

Brush with eggwash and bake at 180°C (350°F) for around 20 minutes. The pastry should be golden brown and the pie should hold its shape when removed from the mould.

1 leek, washed and cut into 1cm (⅜in) dice
3 garlic cloves, minced
150g (5oz) unsalted butter
120g (4oz) flour
100ml (3½ fl oz) Semillon
500g (1lb) black mussels
2 cups milk
2 tablespoons grain mustard
½ cup chopped dill
Black pepper and sea salt, to taste
800g (1½lb) snapper fillet, skinned, boned and cut into large chucks
4 sheets ready-rolled butter puff pastry
Eggwash

sardine fillets in chickpea batter, tomato kasundi

Soak mustard seeds overnight in vinegar. Puree in blender. Add ginger and garlic and blend until smooth.

Halve chillies and remove seeds.

Blanch tomatoes, peel and remove seeds and dice.

Heat oil until smoking. Remove from heat and cool slightly.

Stir in turmeric, cumin and chilli powder. Add garlic and ginger/mustard mix, tomatoes, halved chillies and blended sugar and salt mix. Simmer for about an hour until pulped and oil starts to float on the top. Refrigerate.

Add enough water to besan flour to create a batter.

In a large pot (at least three times the volume of the oil), heat oil to 175°C (350°F).

Dust sardine fillets with flour and then dredge through the chickpea batter to thinly coat and then place into the oil. Fry each fillet for no more than 45 seconds.

Serve with tomato kasundi and some green leaves.

2 tablespoons black mustard seeds
2 cups malt vinegar
250g (8oz) fresh ginger
20 cloves garlic
30 fresh mild large red chillies
2.5kg (5lb) fresh ripe tomatoes
2 tablespoons vegetable oil
2 tablespoons ground turmeric
6 tablespoons ground cumin
2 tablespoons chilli powder
1½ cups sugar
1½ tablespoons salt to taste
150g (5oz) besan flour
12 sardines, butterfly filleted
1½L (48 fl oz) oil for frying, preferably cottonseed

grilled boned quail, salad of shaved fennel, grapes, figs and feta

Using a mandoline or sharp knife, slice fennel bulbs very finely, discarding any tough outer layers and the core. Place in a bowl with rocket and oregano and toss.

Quarter figs, cut grapes in half and add both to the fennel.

Crumble feta into medium sized chunks and add. Drizzle with extra virgin olive oil and vinegar and toss very gently.

Sprinkle sumac over the skin of the boned quail.

In a heavy skillet, cook the quail for two minutes skin side down. Turn and cook for a further two minutes.

Divide the salad between four plates and drizzle over excess dressing. Place a quail skin side up on the salad and serve.

2 medium fennel bulbs
1 handful rocket, washed
½ cup picked oregano
4 figs
1 cup red grapes
160g (5½oz) feta
120ml (4 fl oz) extra virgin olive oil
2 tablespoons red wine vinegar
1 teaspoon ground sumac
4 quails, boned whole

grilled squid and green mango salad

Place garlic, chillies and dried shrimp on a chopping board and chop to a fine mince. Put in a bowl with green mangoes, green beans, tomato, Thai basil, Vietnamese mint, coriander and peanuts.

In a separate bowl, combine fish sauce, lime juice and palm sugar. Warm gently to dissolve. Add dressing to salad and let sit for five minutes.

Heat peanut oil in a wok and sauté the squid, including tentacles, until cooked. Add to salad and toss.

Divide between four bowls and serve sprinkled with fried shallots.

2 cloves garlic
2 small chillies
2 tablespoons dried shrimp
2 green mangoes, peeled and cut into julienne
100g (3½oz) young green beans, sliced finely on an angle
1 ripe tomato, halved, seeded and diced
½ cup picked Thai basil
½ cup picked Vietnamese mint
½ cup picked coriander
2 tablespoons peanuts
2 tablespoons fish sauce
4 tablespoons lime juice
2 tablespoons palm sugar
50ml (1¾ fl oz) peanut oil
500g (1lb) squid, cleaned and cut into strips
3 tablespoons fried shallots

red peanut curry of twice-cooked lamb shank with eggplant

To make the curry paste, roast peppercorns, cumin, coriander, star anise and cinnamon until fragrant and dark, not burnt. Grind in a spice grinder.

Put these and all the ground ingredients down to the paprika through a mincer twice or blend until smooth, adding a little water if necessary.

In a heavy pan with a little oil, brown the lamb shanks. Transfer to a braising pan and add hot stock. Cover and cook in an oven at 170°C (340°F) until tender. Remove and cool.

In a heavy-based frying pan over a high heat, bring coconut cream and vegetable oil to the boil and cook until the oil and the coconut solids separate.

Add the paste, crush lime leaves and add to the pan. Continue stirring to prevent sticking and fry for 15 minutes or so until very fragrant.

Add palm sugar and cook well until caramelised. Add peanuts and stir. Add fish sauce and cook for a further minute, then add coconut milk and bring to the boil. The curry should be very thick with a generous amount of oil floating on top.

Cube the lamb shanks into 2.5cm (1in) pieces, discarding the tendons.

Deep fry in oil until crispy but moist inside, approximately two minutes.

Fold into the curry and serve, garnished with fried shallots, coriander, Vietnamese mint and Thai basil.

1 teaspoon white peppercorns
2 teaspoons cumin seeds
1 teaspoon coriander seeds
6 star anise
3 sticks cinnamon
6 dried long red chillies, split, seeded and ground
12 cloves garlic, chopped and pounded
10 red shallots, chopped and pounded
3 stalks lemongrass, chopped and pounded
2 tablespoons chopped galangal, pounded
4 coriander roots, chopped and pounded
Zest of 1 Kaffir lime, chopped and pounded
1 tablespoon ground paprika
6 lamb shanks
2L (64 fl oz) chicken or veal stock
400ml (13 fl oz) coconut cream
100ml (3½ fl oz) vegetable oil
3 tablespoons shrimp paste, wrapped in foil and grilled until fragrant
6 Kaffir lime leaves
6 tablespoons palm sugar
½ cup roasted peanuts
4 tablespoons fish sauce
250ml (8 fl oz) coconut milk
½ cup fried shallots
½ bunch coriander
½ bunch Vietnamese mint
½ bunch Thai basil

year of the goat curry

Heat some vegetable oil in a large pot and add lime and curry leaves. Cook until fragrant, then add the whole spices and cook until fragrant.

Add onions and cook over a low heat until they are very soft.

Add curry powder and cook until fragrant.

Blitz shallots, ginger, garlic, tomatoes, turmeric, chillies, and coriander roots to a paste, then add to the pot and bring to the simmer.

Add goat meat, turn right down and cover. Stir every 20 minutes or so for two hours.

Remove the lid, add yoghurt and continue to cook for 30–45 minutes.

Add herbs, spring onions and lime juice.

This curry is better left for 24 hours before serving.

Vegetable oil
6 lime leaves
3 branches curry leaves
1 teaspoon fenugreek seeds
1 tablespoon cumin seeds
1 teaspoon fennel seeds
1 teaspoon coriander seeds
1 tablespoon brown mustard seeds
4 dried chillies, whole
3 star anise
1 cinnamon stick
1 tablespoon chilli flakes
6 brown onions, sliced
4 tablespoons Baba's Meat Curry Powder
8 shallots
2 knobs ginger
12 garlic cloves
6 tomatoes
1 knob turmeric
2 birds eye chillies
1 bunch coriander roots
3kg (6lb) diced goat meat
2 cups natural yoghurt
1 bunch Vietnamese mint
1 bunch coriander
½ bunch spring onions, sliced
1 lime

baked idaho potato filled with chorizo and manchego

Wash potatoes well, scrubbing with a brush if necessary. Place on top of rock salt on a baking tray so the potatoes are not in contact with the tray. Bake at 170°C (340°F) for one hour, or until crispy on the outside and soft in the middle.

While the potatoes are baking, dice chorizo and sauté in a little oil. Remove from the heat but leave in the pan.

Cut the tops off the potatoes and scoop out the flesh, being careful not to break through the skins.

Transfer the potato flesh to a bowl and lightly mash with the back of a fork. Spoon in the cooked chorizo sausage and any oil that may have seeped from the chorizo. Add grated manchego cheese, garlic chives, freshly ground black pepper and sea salt.

Return the potatoes to the oven and bake for a further 10 minutes. Serve as a side to grilled steak or fish.

4 russet burbank potatoes
2 cups rock salt
1 chorizo sausage
150g (5oz) manchego cheese, grated
2 tablespoons chopped garlic chives
Black pepper and sea salt, to taste

"As a boy, my grandmother had taught me the art of making tea."

The Art of Making Tea

Blake's Cafeteria

As I mentioned in a previous chapter, I twice ended up starting a new business where I once had been a customer. The first was Tansy's, which we bought off the receivers and reopened as Stella. The second was the iconic Continental Café in Greville Street, Prahran, which became Blake's Cafeteria in November 2001.

The two Marios that owned The Continental Café had been in dispute with their landlord and were unable to secure a new lease. The impending closure of The Conti brought a lot of press and a lot of anger from devotees. Upstairs was a live music venue where many great Australian and overseas acts performed. Downstairs was a café that did eggs and coffee wonderfully, and other standard café fare less well but cheaply.

The Conti was a very successful business with a very passionate following and I would imagine that losing it was like losing a loved one for most of its patrons. I remember reading about the closing of the business and thinking I would hate to be the next operator in that place. Imagine the backlash. A couple of weeks after The Conti closed I got a call from the new leaseholder of the building.

Darren Thornburgh was a nightclub operator who had taken the lease. He was only interested in the upstairs space for a nightclub and was looking for someone to open a café downstairs. We talked and I pondered the idea of having a downmarket food business in much the same mould as The Conti. After all, the business didn't fail, and I liked the energy and style of Greville Street.

Before I made a decision about Greville Street, I put together a series of mock menus simplifying dishes I had done at Blake's or creating new dishes I always wanted to do but didn't have the right vehicle to do so. The menus were my take on what would work in that street for those customers.

I prefer to eat two meals a day: one late morning and one late afternoon. Because I like to eat mid- to late -afternoon I thought that others would also, so the menu was available all day from noon. I had grown to hate the concept of entrée/main/dessert, much preferring to share many plates with my dining companions, so the dishes on my menu were to all be of one size. They would be a bit bigger than an entrée and a bit smaller than a main. The more I developed the concept, the more determined I was to see it come to fruition.

I had no money, but that hadn't been a problem in the past. A friend of ours wanted to get involved in anything I was thinking of doing, so that got rid of 40 per cent of my financing problem. Mum mortgaged her home to partly finance my 60 per cent share so our money problems were solved … temporarily.

Designer Chris Connell's work on casual eateries such as The Melbourne Wine Room and Caffe e Cucina had always impressed me so we engaged Chris to create a smart all-day café to be known as Blake's Cafeteria.

We kept the worn parquetry floor, but pretty much everything else went. The service bar was moved away from the front door, the walls were hard plastered, a couple of rattan screens from W. Pink & Sons were installed to break up the room and a long wooden banquette with padded seats was installed down one wall. Exposed low-watt light bulbs, dangling from retro cords of woven cloth flex, and a communal 80-year-old table from an old munitions factory added to the room's minimalist feel. A triptych from Melbourne artist David Band added a bit of colour to an otherwise dead corner. The tables were mountain ash and the Italian chairs were a beautiful blond woven cane on a brushed aluminium frame.

I gave up drinking coffee a couple of years earlier, so the service of tea was important to me. As a boy, my grandmother had taught me the art of making tea. She always used a Robur teapot that I loved, and even though they cost me $400 each, I bought 12 of them for Cafeteria. Instead of standard café cups and saucers, I bought Koziol Aroma handleless cups from Germany.

We opened and the place was instantly busy. I knew we would never be able to win over the old Conti diehards and sure enough, they made their disappointments known in no uncertain terms. But we brought many new customers to Greville Street and business was good—until we hit licensing problems.

The original licence covered two floors by the one operator, so the new licence had to be divided for two different businesses. It became a nightmare. We thought we were operating legally but on a routine check by local police, it was discovered that we were in fact in breach of our licence. All sales of alcoholic beverages were to cease immediately, and Cafeteria was to remain completely dry until the mess was sorted out. We lost 90 per cent of our evening trade and were forced to close at 4pm until we got our licence back. Not only did we lose a lot of money in those three weeks, we also lost momentum. It is very hard to reclaim customers that you have lost.

Then my business world fell apart. Blake's Restaurant at Southgate had its locks changed by the landlord after I missed my rent payments. I had put Blake's money into Cafeteria and had to draw down part of my shareholding to start paying off debts. My creditors were mostly small business people who could not afford to lose money through bad debts. If I ever wanted to do business in my town again, I had to make a commitment to repay them. Running away to Mumbai with creditors' money, as another high-profile Melbourne chef had done, was not an option!

For some reason I thought that Cafeteria should have two head chefs. We were doing breakfast, lunch and dinner seven days a week, so I needed to find two chefs that had the right demeanour to share the responsibilities; where their individual strengths and weaknesses would combine well. The two head chef thing worked really well, but I think more so because of the two chefs involved. Daniel Wilson had worked for me for a couple of years at Blake's, but had never run a kitchen before. Emma Mackay was a gun pastry chef but had never done pan work. They combined brilliantly and their work culminated in them being co-awarded The Age 'Young Chef of the Year' in our first year of operation. I don't think the partnership would have worked anywhere near as well with any two other chefs; egos and temperaments would make it impossible. On this occasion though, I was lucky.

Cafeteria was given a chef's hat by *The Age Good Food Guide*—a bit of a surprise for an all-day café. The awards ceremony that year was a bittersweet occasion. It had only been three weeks since Blake's had closed down and I had so much going on in my head.

At the time I felt like the little boy with his fingers in the dyke. So many people to deal with, suppliers to appease, staff to placate, stock to return: just so much explaining to do. But most importantly I had to reconcile how I brought this all upon myself.

It was a particularly disheartening time. I had managed to survive some close scrapes over the previous 10 years, but now it seemed like the end of my restaurant life as I knew it. I was married to my restaurant and having it taken away from me immediately left a huge void in my life.

At a time when I needed home to be a sanctuary, it became as much a nightmare as the rest of my life. And again it was all my doing. Our relationship was failing but my business life was even more of a mess, so I let the marriage meander. Mischee was so buried in our children that she was either oblivious to the shortcomings of our marriage or she just hoped that everything would turn out fine as it had in the past. I began an affair with a staff member and we fell in love. Mischee and I separated.

Sharen and I had the most wonderful 18 months together before she felt the need to leave. She needed a Jewish husband to start a family, and this gentile had already been there and done that … twice. She moved overseas and in the process broke my heart, though I can now look back and say that she did the right thing by both of us.

Sharen leaving forced me to get my life together. I moved into a small apartment and hid myself away. I was partly wallowing in self-pity but mostly I was bringing some much-needed discipline into my life. This was sink or swim.

I had talks with a fellow restaurateur and long-lunch mate, Fab Nicolao, about taking over the catering for Gold Class Cinemas. Fab was in much the same position as me, only he still had his struggling restaurant and I had lost mine. I developed a concept menu for Gold Class and conducted a tasting at Cafeteria for a swag couple of Village Cinema executives. We won a three-year contract and Foodmeisters Inc was formed.

The food was not what you might expect Andrew Blake to be involved with, but then Gold Class is a blue-collar experience and it's no use giving patrons something they don't want. We made wontons, samosas, sausage rolls, pizzas and chips among other things, but we did them well and all by hand.

Before we took over, a random portion of commercially mass-produced spiced wedges would be scattered on an oven tray, baked for 12 minutes and served. We hand cut potatoes into wedges, blanched them in a combi-steamer oven, then refreshed and packaged them into 400 gram portions for delivery to each site. We installed small bench-top fryers in each cinema kitchenette and taught the cinema 'cooks' how to finish them off. It would now take just three to four minutes to present a superior product rather than 12 minutes for an inferior one. We also imported wood-fired pizza bases from Italy.

I will never forget Fab's mum coming into the kitchen on our first day of production. We had potato gnocchi with veal ragu on the menu. In walks this Italian momma in her sixties, resplendent in fur coat, immaculately coiffed hair and hands full of rings, saying, 'I will make the gnocchi.' Off came the coat and rings, up went the sleeves and Mrs Nicolao whipped up 10 kilograms of the softest potato gnocchi known to man.

Foodmeisters Inc only supplied the cinemas at Crown to start with, but quickly rolled it out to seven other sites across Melbourne. Fab and I were also on a year's contract with Village Cinemas to oversee the roll out and train staff at each venue. As we trained staff while we were out delivering, we didn't have any need to employ anyone else. We both had restaurant debts, so any money we could save we did. If that meant driving a delivery van for a year, then so be it.

It was while I was making a delivery and training staff at Southland that I received a very unexpected call. It was from a former customer whose family had been very good friends of Blake's Restaurant, having eaten there probably three Sundays a month for the previous couple of years. I hadn't seen Mr X for a while—it had been a year since Blake's had closed—and after exchanging niceties, he got to the point. He had heard that I was doing it tough and wanted to take me out for lunch to discuss my predicament.

We met at Koko, a Japanese restaurant housed in and owned by Crown, and I told him what had happened and where I was at. What he proposed completely overwhelmed me.

'Blakey, I have been very fortunate in my life and would like to help you out,' he said. 'I remember you taking meals from your restaurant into the hospital when Mrs X was expecting, and when you got me tickets for the grand final a couple of years ago. Those gestures I haven't forgotten.'

He asked how much I owed, which I estimated at around $170,000. I actually owed a lot more but couldn't bring myself to say the real amount.

'I am going to deposit the money in your bank account next week, and if I don't see it again, it won't matter.'

It was as simple and straightforward as that. I can't mention this man's name, but his generosity allowed me to clear a substantial amount of debt and, more importantly, to move on from the monster that I had created. One day I will knock on this man's door with an envelope to repay my debt, but I can never repay my gratitude.

Cafeteria got into financial problems, partly because I drew down my loan account too far for the business to be able to afford, and partly because the business model that I had set up was flawed. The business went into receivership, my partner took over and before long, I was gone.

Daniel Wilson & Emma Mackay (2002)

"Cafeteria was given a chef's hat by The Age Good Food Guide — a bit of a surprise for an all-day cafe."

wagyu beef chipolatas with bubble'n'squeak and tomato jam

Place tomatoes, garlic, onion and ginger in a saucepan and simmer for 30 minutes, stirring occasionally. Add lemon juice and sugar and continue cooking slowly until the tomato mixture becomes jam-like.

Cook potatoes in simmering water. When tender, drain and mash.

Add cabbage, peas, corn, parsley, sea salt and freshly ground black pepper. Mix well and form into patties.

Melt butter in a non-stick fry pan and cook the patties a couple of minutes each side or until golden brown.

Grill sausages and serve with bubble'n'squeak and tomato jam.

1kg (2lb) ripe Roma tomatoes, chopped
2 garlic cloves, finely sliced
1 medium brown onion, finely sliced
1 knob ginger, peeled and cut into threads
Juice of one lemon
3 tablespoons sugar
400g (13oz) potatoes, peeled
1 cup sliced cabbage, cooked
½ cup peas, cooked
½ cup corn kernels, cooked
2 tablespoons chopped parsley
Sea salt and black pepper, to taste
25g (⅘oz) butter
16 wagyu beef chipolatas

thyme-roasted portobello mushrooms with brioche, pecorino and pesto

Place basil, garlic, parmesan, pinenuts and olive oil in a food processor and pulse a couple of times. Scrape down sides and pulse a couple more times. The pesto should not be completely pureed, rather a chunky paste. Transfer to a bowl and thin with a little more olive oil if necessary.

Clean mushrooms, sprinkle with some thyme leaves and sea salt. Drizzle with oil and roast at 180°C (350°F) until just cooked.

Cut four thick slices of brioche and toast.

When mushrooms are cooked, remove from oven and drizzle each with pesto. Then top each with shaved pecorino.

Stack three mushrooms up on each slice of toasted brioche and serve.

1 bunch basil, picked, washed and dried
1 garlic clove, roughly chopped
100g (3½oz) parmesan, grated
50g (1¾oz) pinenuts
120ml (4 fl oz) extra virgin olive oil
12 Portobello mushrooms
2 teaspoons thyme leaves
Sea salt, to taste
1 loaf brioche
80g (2⅘oz) shaved pecorino

pan-fried barramundi with whipped taramasalata, grilled salad onions and black olive oil

Spoon yoghurt onto a large square of muslin cloth and tie up to create a sack. Hang the sack overnight in a refrigerator to drain excess liquid.

Squeeze excess water out of bread and place in food processor with tarama, garlic and three-quarters of the lemon juice. Blitz to a smooth paste and slowly add the oils.

Transfer the taramasalata to a bowl and add the drained yoghurt and freshly ground black pepper. Whip together and season to taste.

Pit olives and blend in a food processor, drizzling in olive oil to create a thin paste.

Trim salad onions of their tops so that 5–7.5cm (2–3in) are left of the small bulb and stem. Cut the salad onions in half lengthways.

In a heavy skillet, with a little olive oil, pan-fry the salad onions cut side down until golden brown. Turn over and place in a moderate oven (180°C, 350°F) until cooked but firm.

Pan-fry barramundi evenly on both sides until just cooked.

Place barramundi in the centre of each plate, crispy skin side up. Shape quenelles of taramasalata and place on the barramundi. Place two halves of grilled salad onion cut side up on the taramasalata. Drizzle around a little of the black olive oil and serve.

175ml (6 fl oz) yoghurt
3 slices of bread, crust removed and soaked in water or milk
100g (3½oz) tarama
1 garlic clove
Juice of 2 lemons
150ml (5¼fl oz) olive oil
75ml (2¾ fl oz) vegetable oil
Black pepper, to taste
100g (3½oz) Kalamata olives
100ml (3½ fl oz) extra virgin olive oil
4 salad onions
4 x 120g (4oz) pieces of barramundi

beetroot and vodka-cured ocean trout with goat's cheese fritters, soft herbs and sour cream

Remove all pin bones from ocean trout fillet with tweezers or pointy-nose pliers.

Mix rock salt and sugar together in a bowl. Add dill and peppercorns.

Roughly chop beetroot and blitz in the work bowl of a food processor. Add puree to rock salt mixture, along with vodka. Mix well.

Spread half the mixture on a small tray and place the ocean trout fillet skin side up on top. Spread remaining mixture over the skin of the fish and place another tray on top. Weigh the top tray down with a few jars or tins. Cure for eight hours.

When cured sufficiently, wash fillet under cold running water, pat dry, wrap in plastic wrap and refrigerate.

Peel potatoes and cover with cold water, add a pinch of salt and bring to the boil. Simmer until soft, strain off all the water and mash the potatoes.

Place 200ml (6½ fl oz) water, butter and a pinch of salt and pepper into a saucepan. Bring to the boil gradually over a low heat.

Once the mixture has come to the boil add flour. Stir, still over a low heat, until the mixture comes away from the sides of the pan.

Remove from the heat and, while continually stirring, add one egg at a time. Allow to cool.

Fold the mashed potatoes into this mix, and then fold in grated goat's cheese.

Deep fry tablespoon-sized portions of the mix at 170°C (340°F) until golden brown.

Thinly slice the cured ocean trout and arrange on plates. Scatter with micro herbs and dot with ½ teaspoon dobs of sour cream. Place a goat's cheese fritter in the centre and serve.

1 fillet ocean trout
500g (1lb) rock salt
440g (14½oz) sugar
½ cup chopped dill
2 tablespoons crushed white peppercorns
3 medium beetroot
100ml (3½ fl oz) vodka
400g (13oz) potatoes
60g (2oz) butter
80g (2⅘oz) flour
2 eggs
170g (5½oz) aged goat's cheese
½ cup assorted picked micro herbs
Sour cream

world's best-practice chicken schnitzel, eggplant pickle

Soak chillies in hot water until soft, about 30 minutes. Drain, but reserve water.

Using a food processor, blend chillies, garlic, ginger, turmeric and mustard seeds into a paste with a little chilli water.

Cut eggplants into large chunks, about 2cm (¾in) square.

Heat oil in a frying pan, then add spice paste and stir for a few minutes to release flavours. Add eggplant and cook until soft. Add palm sugar, salt and vinegar and simmer over low heat until thick. Add garam masala off the heat and cool.

Tear bread, crust and all, into large chunks. Blitz in a food processor to make coarse breadcrumbs. Do not overprocess—chunky crumbs are best! Add lemon zest and mix well.

With each chicken breast, fold out the fillet from the breast and flatten lightly between two sheets of plastic wrap.

Season with sea salt and freshly ground black pepper, dust with flour, dip in the eggwash and crumb well.

Heat oil and butter in a large pan over medium heat until the butter starts to foam. Cook the crumbed breasts two at a time until golden brown and crispy on both sides.

Serve with a generous spoonful of eggplant pickle.

6 large dried chillies
1 tablespoon minced garlic
2 teaspoons minced ginger
1 teaspoon ground turmeric
1 tablespoon brown mustard seeds
500g (1lb) small eggplants
200ml (6½ fl oz) vegetable oil
65g (2oz) palm sugar
2 teaspoons sea salt
100ml (3½ fl oz) malt vinegar
1 teaspoon garam masala
1 loaf one-day-old bread
Finely grated zest of 2 lemons
2 eggs
½ cup milk
4 free-range chicken breasts
Black pepper and sea salt, to taste
1 cup flour
½ cup olive oil
30g (1oz) butter

pan-seared red mullet fillets with wild rocket, romesco sauce and grilled turkish bread

Toast almonds in a heavy pan over medium heat until golden, about three minutes. Transfer almonds to food processor.

Place bread in the same skillet and cook until lightly toasted, about one minute per side.

Tear bread into pieces and add to processor. With the motor running, drop garlic through feed tube and pulse until almonds and garlic are finely processed. Add red peppers, oil, vinegar and cayenne pepper and process until mixture is the consistency of thick mayonnaise, scraping down sides of bowl occasionally. Put aside.

Fillet red mullet and remove all small bones with pointy-nose pliers or tweezers.

Wash wild rocket twice, changing the water between each wash. Dry completely in a salad spinner.

Cut Turkish bread into rectangles of 10cm x 5cm (4in x 2in). Brush with olive oil and grill in the heavy pan.

Lightly oil the pan and sear the red mullet fillets for 20 seconds each side, starting skin side up. Season lightly after turning over. Remove from heat.

Place a piece of grilled Turkish bread on the centre of each plate. Top generously with leaves of rocket. Place two fillets of red mullet on each, and spoon on Romesco sauce.

2 tablespoons slivered almonds
1 thin slice French bread
1 large garlic clove
2 red peppers, roasted and peeled
2 tablespoons Spanish olive oil
1 tablespoon red wine vinegar
¼ teaspoon cayenne pepper
6 red mullet
50g (1¾oz) wild rocket
1 medium Turkish bread loaf

tuna tartare with pequillo peppers and grilled sourdough

Cut tuna into 6mm (¼in) dice and place in a bowl with chilli, garlic, shallots, coriander, peanut oil and lime juice. Season with plenty of freshly cracked black pepper and a little sea salt. Let sit for five minutes, tossing occasionally.

Brush bread with olive oil and grill on a low to medium barbeque.

Spoon tuna tartare into pequillo peppers.

Place two peppers on each piece of toast and serve.

500g (1lb) sashimi-quality yellowfin tuna
1 birds eye chilli, seeded and minced
1 clove garlic, minced
2 red shallots, minced
3 tablespoons chopped coriander
4 tablespoons fragrant peanut oil
2 tablespoons lime juice
Black pepper and sea salt, to taste
4 slices crusty sourdough bread
Extra virgin olive oil
8 pequillo peppers

barbeque moreton bay bugs

sweetfish sauce, mint and coriander

barbeque moreton bay bugs, sweetfish sauce, mint and coriander

Shave palm sugar and heat gently to a syrup, using a little water to help the syrup form.

Add Kaffir lime leaves, red shallots, coriander root, lemongrass and galangal. Simmer until the syrup thickens and darkens a little.

Add tamarind and fish sauce and simmer a further two minutes to incorporate. Strain and cool.

Remove the heads and cut the bug tails in half lengthways. Brush the cut side with a little peanut oil and barbeque.

When cooked transfer to a platter. Drizzle liberally with sweetfish sauce. Garnish with lots of young mint and coriander, chilli and both shallots. Squeeze lime juice over and serve.

300g (10oz) palm sugar
6 Kaffir lime leaves
3 red shallots, sliced
6 coriander roots
1 stalk lemongrass, smashed
1 knob galangal, sliced
60g (2oz) tamarind, mixed to a pulp with 50ml (1¾ fl oz) water
75ml (2¾ fl oz) fish sauce
3kg (6lb) raw Moreton Bay bugs
Peanut oil
1 cup mint leaves
1 cup picked coriander
1 chilli, deseeded and sliced
2 red shallots, sliced
4 tablespoons fried shallots
1–2 limes

kentucky fried quail with vietnamese slaw

Combine all spice mix ingredients and set aside.

In a bowl, mix all dressing ingredients well so as to dissolve the palm sugar.

Toss all salad ingredients in another bowl.

Bone quails out in one piece, leaving in the leg and wing bones.

Heat peanut oil in a fry pan or wok to a temperature of 170°C (340°F).

Dust quails lightly with plain flour, dunk in buttermilk and then dredge through the spice mix, coating well and evenly and patting lightly to remove any excess.

Fry quails for about three or four minutes until crust is golden to medium brown and the quail flesh is pink.

Put a small mound of Vietnamese slaw on the centre of each plate and top with a splayed whole fried quail.

spice mix
3 teaspoons ground coriander
3 teaspoons ground cumin
1 teaspoon cayenne
3 teaspoons sweet paprika
2 teaspoons salt
1 teaspoon five spice
1 teaspoon dried oregano
1 teaspoon dried thyme
2 teaspoons garlic powder
2 teaspoons onion powder
3 teaspoons ground szechwan pepper
2 teaspoons ground white pepper
8 tablespoons plain flour

dressing
1 teaspoon minced garlic
1 teaspoon minced ginger
2 tablespoons fish sauce
100ml (3½ fl oz) lime juice
100ml (3½ fl oz) rice wine vinegar
75g (2¾oz) palm sugar, shaved

salad
½ Chinese cabbage, shredded
1 carrot, cut into julienne
4 red shallots, finely sliced
1 birds eye chilli, seeded and finely sliced
½ cup picked Vietnamese mint
½ cup picked coriander
50g (1¾oz) toasted peanuts

quail
4 quails
500ml (16 fl oz) peanut oil
¾ cup buttermilk

baby pavlova, strawberries, crystallised rose petals, raspberry sauce and rose syrup

Beat eggwhites until they begin to hold their shape. Add half the caster sugar and beat for three minutes at high speed. Add the remaining sugar and beat for a further three minutes at high speed.

Add cornflour, vinegar and vanilla and mix in on low speed.

Cut four strips of baking paper 20cm (8in) long and 5cm (2in) wide. Form each strip into a ring and tape the ends together. Place each 'collar' on an oven tray lined with baking paper.

Pipe or spoon the meringue into each collar and cook at 120°C (250°F) for one hour. Turn off the oven and leave the pavlovas inside for 30 minutes.

Combine the caster sugar, one cup of water, rosewater and petals in a saucepan and bring to a boil. Simmer for five-10 minutes to a light syrup and cool. Strain and reserve.

In a small saucepan, crush the raspberries with the back of a large spoon. Add sugar and simmer for a couple of minutes. Cool and strain through a fine sieve, adding lemon juice to taste.

Wash the rose petals very gently in cold water. Drain and let dry.

Whisk the eggwhite a little to loosen. Hold each rose petal with tweezers and coat with eggwhite, using a small brush. Sprinkle lightly with sugar and lay on baking paper to dry. Store in an airtight container until required.

Top each mini pavlova with a generous dollop of whipped cream. Arrange strawberries on top of each, then spoon over a little rose syrup and raspberry sauce. Finally, place six crystallised rose petals on top.

meringue
4 egg whites
250g (8oz) caster sugar
2 teaspoons cornflour
1 teaspoon vinegar
1 teaspoon vanilla extract

rose syrup
1 cup caster sugar
1 tablespoons rosewater
1 small handful rose petals

raspberry sauce
1 punnet raspberries
2 tablespoons caster sugar
lemon juice, to taste

crystallised rose petals
24 very small rose petals
1 eggwhite
½ cup caster sugar

300ml (10 fl oz) whipped cream, to serve
1 punnet strawberries, to serve

solomon island honey ice-cream sandwich with gold leaf florentines

Combine milk and cream in a saucepan and bring to a boil.

Whisk egg yolks and honey in a bowl until incorporated.

Add the milk/cream mixture to the eggs and cook out over a double boiler until the custard thickens and coats the back of a spoon.

Chill immediately over a slurry of ice water, strain and churn in an ice-cream machine according to the manufacturer's instructions.

Line four metal or plastic rings (approx 8cm (3in) in diameter and 2.5cm (1in) deep) on a tray with plastic wrap. Pour in the churned ice-cream to create ice cream discs and fold over the plastic wrap flaps to fully enclose. Freeze.

Preheat the oven to 180°C (350°F). Brush a baking tray with oil.

Combine flour, nuts and fruit together in a bowl.

Heat butter, golden syrup and brown sugar together in a saucepan until the sugar has dissolved. Add the wet mixture to the dry mixture and incorporate thoroughly.

Spoon dollops of the mixture onto the oiled baking trays and press into circles, allowing room for the dough to spread. Bake for seven–eight minutes.

Remove from the oven, leaving the Florentines on the tray to cool and crisp before transferring to a rack.

Drizzle or pipe melted chocolate onto the top of every second Florentine and place fragments of gold leaf on the chocolate as it sets.

Wet sugar with enough water to make a liquid. Over a medium heat, caramelise to a golden brown colour and add cream, being careful to avoid splashing on skin.

Reduce heat and cook for a further three minutes or until a saucing thickness has been reached. Cool.

Unwrap the ice-cream discs and sandwich between two Florentines, with the gold leaf ones on top and plain ones underneath. Drizzle a little caramel sauce on each plate and top with the ice-cream sandwich.

250ml (8 fl oz) milk
250ml (8 fl oz) cream
6 egg yolks
180g (6oz) Solomon Island honey
4 tablespoons vegetable oil
½ cup flour
3 tablespoons chopped almonds
3 tablespoons chopped macadamias
3 tablespoons chopped pistachios
3 tablespoons chopped mixed peel
3 tablespoons dried cranberries
60g (2oz) butter
1 tablespoon golden syrup
½ cup brown sugar
100g (3½oz) chocolate, melted
1 sheet gold leaf
1 cup sugar
300ml (10 fl oz) cream, warmed

"She wanted me to explore the possibility of a dog café, not just a dog-friendly cafe, but a cafe where dogs came first and their owners came second."

Blake's Feast

Blake's Feast

Blake's Feast began its life as an incarnation of Kanis, Blake & Kanis in 1992. When Jennie and I separated, I left KBK to concentrate on the impending opening of Blake's at Southgate and the Kanis cousins were well and truly over it. Jennie made an offer to buy KBK and the boys couldn't get out quickly enough.

Jennie ran Blake's Feast as a providore and wholesaler for a number of years, before closing the retail and just doing wholesale. In 2002 she was approached by a board member of The Malthouse Theatre at Southbank, with the idea of taking over the café and catering there. While I wasn't involved in any sense with Blake's Feast, Jennie asked me what I thought and if I might be interested in setting up a catering company there with her.

The Malthouse has always been a great venue and under the direction of Michael Kantor, the theatre went through something of a renaissance after a dwindling subscriber base had left attendances well down. Of what we saw, the food offering was very ordinary and in need of some love and care. We signed a three-year lease and Blake's Feast became a catering company.

While I did help set up Blake's Feast, I wasn't actually working for the company. I was doing my Foodmeisters Inc thing for Village Cinemas and winding down from Cafeteria when Jennie suggested I come in part-time. She was running the business with her daughter, Kasey, who had come in on a needs basis. I started developing new menus, meeting with potential clients to sell functions and helping put together tenders to win new contracts. It was all very new to me, but I had confidence in my product, and no-one is better at selling my food than me.

Old mate Glenby was head chef at Damm Fine Food but over lunch with Jennie he voiced his frustration at not being offered a share of the business as had long been discussed. During the second bottle of wine Jennie offered him a share of ours as enticement to come back to the fold.

Blake's Feast was still a very small catering company and we couldn't afford for both Jennie and I to be full-time. But in 2005 she accepted an offer to manage and run Cammeray Waters, a conferencing property just outside Woodend, which in turn meant I could move into Blake's Feast full-time. That might not sound like a big deal, but to me it was very important. My confidence was pretty low at the time and I was not sure how to get out of it. I had been living a very low-key, frugal existence and was going through the process of changing my life. I would get home from work and thoughtfully cook dinner for myself before opening up the laptop to finish quotes or respond to non-stop enquiries. I was burying myself in my work and it was a good place to be. Blake's Feast offered me security at a time when I needed it.

We'd never tendered for any contracts before, but realised if we were to grow beyond word-of-mouth, then we had to. Our first successful tender was for The Royal Botanic Gardens in Melbourne and the about-to-be-opened Australian Native Gardens in Cranbourne. The Melbourne gardens have been great. Blake's Feast has sole rights to all catering on the Old Observatory Buildings, lawns, pavilions and marquees, and also coordinate every wedding ceremony held in the gardens. Some Saturdays in January host up to 15 wedding ceremonies, so staff are kept very busy.

The next contract we picked up was at Mt Hotham, where the operators of Zirky's had gone bust the previous season. Operating a 45-seat café, 65-seat restaurant and 125-seat bistro so far from Melbourne was always going to be difficult, at least until we got to know the nuances of snow businesses. The kitchen at Zirky's was, and still is, appalling. There was no way we would be able to produce all the food necessary out of this little kitchen on bottled gas.

Hotham management were to fly Kasey and I up to Dinner Plain for a look over the facility. As we walked across the tarmac at Essendon Airfields, Kasey saw that we were going by light plane and started weeping and shaking uncontrollably. The pilot said that driving back to the city on the freeway was far more dangerous than flying to Hotham, but she wouldn't have a bar of it and I flew alone. I have no idea what she thought we were flying in, but a light plane didn't do it for her.

I sourced a refrigerated transport company that would pick food up from our kitchen in Melbourne and drop it off at the base of the snowfields where Hotham Freight would complete the journey. The kitchen spent a couple of days making a tonne and a half of stocks, soups, braises, sauces and everything else we had worked out should come from Melbourne. Glenby had the food stacked on pallets at 10am when we had arranged for the pick-up. The driver showed up five hours later and without a hydraulic tailgate to load the pallets. We were going to have to unload everything and hand-load onto the back of the truck.

The truck driver was told, in no uncertain words, that we would deliver the food ourselves. So the next day our delivery van was loaded to the gunnels and delivered by one our kitchen hands right to Zirky's door. It worked a treat and we have sent our van up every week of every season since.

When we took over we wanted to get rid of the bain-marie bistro in favour of some quality short order pub food. I'm glad we didn't because customers queue out into the snow to get our hearty soups, stews, braises and curries.

In 2004 I was contacted by Jane Brook, a friend whose company did PR for Mars Petcare. She wanted me to explore the possibility of a 'dog café'—not just a dog-friendly café, but a café where dogs came first and their owners came second. The café would operate for four months over summer and was supposed to be a thank you to My Dog customers for their brand loyalty.

Jane came upon a site on Station Pier in Port Melbourne that had heritage listing as an old ferry ticketing booth and waiting room. I filed all the necessary forms with the Port Phillip Council Health Department and, after much to-ing and fro-ing, got the permits through. It was only when the head of the department came back from extended leave that he told me we were very lucky indeed to have been granted the permit. I fancy that someone received a 'please explain' from within the council department.

The dining area had eight large tables and 32 chairs. Each table had a 'doggy day bed' along with fun features such as a larger-than-life sculpture of Imelda and a three-tiered water fountain. Our cooking equipment consisted of a toaster, a microwave, an electric fry pan and a bottled gas burner.

I had to do a crash course on what dogs could and couldn't eat, and came up with a small menu of dishes that were closely aligned with the My Dog range. We offered delicacies such as braised beef cheek, oxtail ragout, slow-cooked lamb shanks, chicken livers with bacon and bone marrow dog biscuits. Rather decadent for a dog at $5 for a 100 gram portion, but then dog-lovers are a breed apart. One of my suppliers at Prahran Market has a customer that buys fillet steak for her dog and mince for herself.

On the human side, I had fun developing a menu of flippant items like Special K-9, Border Collie Flower Soup, German Shepherd's Pie, Great Dane ish Pastries and Boxer Chocolates.

In 2007, Blake's Feast submitted a tender for The Melbourne Sports & Aquatic Centre. This was one contract that we were very keen to get, and not just because it was a valuable one. I take my children there periodically so I was fully aware of the shortcomings of the product. To my mind, a sports centre has a responsibility to have a mostly healthy menu on offer and the existing caterer's product range was appalling.

We didn't get the MSAC contract, but as long as the new caterer's offering was substantially better than their predecessor's, I would have been satisfied, even happy. I went back for a look after the new caterer had settled in, only to be dismayed at the sameness on offer. The powers that be at MSAC had the chance to change the junk food culture but they didn't. There has to be a balance between filling your coffers and providing your clients with a nutritious, healthy menu.

Blake's Feast will continue to be honest in our approach to tendering, at the expense of missing out on contracts where money means more than menu and service. We won't be playing the game.

At the end of 2008 we decided against taking up a three-year option on our lease at The Malthouse. As in any relationship, needs change and goalposts move. We enjoyed our time at The Malt, but our wages were high, margins low, and we had been asked by management to stay open until after the show was finished which just wasn't doable. The decision not to renew was an important change in policy. In the past, we just wanted to do business. Now, we will only do business if we feel it is going to be good for Blake's Feast.

Our corporate and private business has been growing remarkably, even through the global financial crisis. I am still cooking for weddings at the Royal Botanic Gardens, boardroom lunches and small dinners in clients' houses, and will continue to do so until I am physically unable. We are about to embark on a relationship with Rylands Independent Retirement Living, operating the food and beverage at a number of their luxury facilities.

My daughter Neredah has joined Blake's Feast full-time in a bookkeeping and business development role. Jennie has also rejoined, taking care of contract management. Both will be seen from time to time serving customers at functions, alongside Kasey, with Glenby and I cooking. That is the nature of Blake's Feast, which dictates we all have to multiskill. I have never worked as hard as I do now. At an age where I should be spending more time on the golf course, I find myself too busy to play as often as I once did.

I am not out of the poo just yet. I still have some debts from the carnage but I am not far from clearing them. But for all I have been through, I wouldn't change a thing if it meant not being where I am right now. I love going to work because I work with the people I love. When I look up from my desk and see my girls, you just can't imagine how happy I am, remembering that as a wild young chef working long hours I was frequently absent.

I look back on my career and know I am fortunate to have been able to realise my dreams, even if some of them were to become my nightmares. I have worked hard, fucked up, had fun, been broke, been hurt and hurt others. I believe the journey is far more important than the destination. I have nothing tangible to show for my life's work but that has never been important to me. Like the tall skinny bloke at the end of the spaghetti westerns, I am riding off into the sunset, content that I have survived.

"I am still cooking for weddings at the RBG, boardroom lunches and small dinners in client's houses, and will continue to do so until I am physically unable."

Kasey's wedding photo: Jasper, Claudette, Mischee, Steve, Kasey, Neredah, myself & Jennie (2008)

crayfish club sandwich

Dissolve brown sugar in water to create a syrup.

Lay kaiserfleisch slices on an oven tray and brush with the syrup. Bake at 180°C (350°F) until the kaiserfleisch caramelises.

Remove the tail meat from the crayfish in one large piece and slice finely, laying out on a plate as you go.

Cut crusts off bread and toast both sides.

To construct, thinly spread mayo on two slices of toast. Top one with some lettuce and tomato slices. Place two kaiserfleisch rashers on the tomato, then some thin slices of crayfish. Season with sea salt and freshly ground black pepper to taste. Place other slice of toast on top and cut in half.

2 tablespoons brown sugar
4 tablespoons water
10 thin slices kaiserfleisch
1 small freshly cooked crayfish
10 slices white toasting bread
¼ cup mayonnaise
1 young cos lettuce, washed and outer leaves discarded
2 ripe tomatoes, finely sliced
Sea salt and black pepper, to taste

quail saltimbocca on hummus crouton

Soak chickpeas in water for a minimum of six hours. Drain, cover with fresh water and bring to the boil. Simmer and skim regularly until the chickpeas are tender.

Drain and place in a food processor with garlic, lemon juice and tahini. Blitz to a smooth paste, adding olive oil and a little water to adjust the consistency. Season and add more water if necessary as hummus cools and thickens.

Very lightly, butter both sides of the croutons and bake at 175°C (350°F) until golden brown.

Cut each slice of prosciutto in half lengthways and crossways. Place a sage leaf on each quail breast and wrap the quail and sage with a piece of prosciutto.

Pan-fry both sides of the wrapped quail breasts in a little olive oil to seal, then place in an oven at 160°C (325°F) for five minutes. Take out and rest in a warm place for a couple of minutes.

Generously spread hummus on each crouton. Cut each quail breast in half on a slight angle and place a half cut-side up on each crouton.

1 cup cooked chickpeas
2 garlic cloves
Juice of 1 lemon
100ml (3½ fl oz) tahini
3 tablespoons extra virgin olive oil
2 tablespoons unsalted butter, softened
10 croutons, cut from a ficelle or small baguette
5 small sage leaves
2 fine slices prosciutto
5 quail breasts

gazpacho shots with blueswimmer crabmeat and basil oil

Roughly chop peppers, cucumber, garlic, onion and tomatoes and puree with a bar blender or hand-held blender. Add vinegar and adjust the mixture with a little tomato juice if necessary to make a soupy consistency. Season to taste with sea salt and freshly ground black pepper and chill.

Carefully fill shot glasses three-quarters of the way with chilled gazpacho. Add a small amount of crabmeat to each shot glass and drizzle a small amount of basil oil over.

½ **green pepper**
½ **red pepper**
¼ **continental cucumber**
2 garlic cloves
½ **Spanish onion**
3 overripe tomatoes
3 tablespoons sherry vinegar
Sea salt and black pepper, to taste
100g (3½oz) picked blue-swimmer crabmeat
2 tablespoons basil oil

pea and prosciutto arancini, molten gorgonzola

Sweat onion and garlic in butter and olive oil. Add arborio rice and continue cooking without colouring for one minute.

Add white wine, cook for one minute and then add half the chicken stock.

When absorbed add the remaining chicken stock. When almost absorbed and rice almost cooked, add mashed peas and diced prosciutto and incorporate.

When rice is fully cooked, add chopped parsley, season and remove from heat. Spread risotto on a tray and cool.

Shape the risotto into balls slightly smaller than a golf ball. Dice gorgonzola and press a small dice into the centre of each arancini, re-shaping to form perfectly round balls with the gorgonzola in the middle.

Tear bread up, crusts and all, and blitz in a food processor to make breadcrumbs.

Roll each arancini in flour, then dredge through an eggwash and coat with the breadcrumbs.

Heat the oil to 170°C (340°F) and fry the arancini until golden brown and crispy. Serve immediately while the gorgonzola is molten.

1 small onion, finely diced
2 garlic cloves, minced
30g (1oz) unsalted butter
2 tablespoons olive oil
¾ cup arborio rice
½ cup white wine
3 cups light chicken stock, hot
1 cup cooked peas
80g (2⅘oz) prosciutto, cut into 5mm (¼in) dice
¼ cup chopped flat-leaf parsley
100g (3½oz) gorgonzola
1 loaf of day-old bread
1 cup flour
Eggwash
1L (32 fl oz) cottonseed oil

ras el hanout spiced duck and quince mini pies

Sprinkle two tablespoons ras el hanout over duck legs and rub in to coat evenly. Refrigerate for 24 hours to infuse flavours before cooking.

Sear the duck legs in a heavy pan with a little oil and then roast in an oven for 50 minutes at 160°C (325°F). Cool the duck legs, shred the meat off the bones and put aside.

Sweat garlic and shallots in unsalted butter for one minute over a medium heat. Add one teaspoon ras el hanout and sweat a further minute.

Add the shredded duck meat and demi-glaze and simmer for a minute or two until the sauce is mostly absorbed. Remove from the heat and stir through the diced quince. Adjust seasoning and cool.

With a pastry cutter, cut the rolled short-crust pastry into rounds big enough to line the indents on a mini muffin tray.

Spray the indents with a non-stick spray and line each indent with short crust pastry dough. Press in well and trim.

Spoon in the duck/quince mixture and top with a round of puff pastry cut to fit. Brush lids with eggwash and sprinkle with black sesame seeds.

Bake at 170°C (340°F) for around 15 minutes or until pastry is golden brown and cooked. Garnish each pie with a picked coriander leaf.

2 tablespoons ras el hanout
2 duck legs
1 clove garlic, minced
2 shallots, minced
20g (²⁄₃oz) unsalted butter
1 teaspoon ras el hanout
80ml (2¾ fl oz) demi-glaze
80g (2⅘oz) poached quince, cut into 5mm (¼in) dice
2 sheets ready-rolled shortcrust pastry
1 sheet ready-rolled butter puff pastry
Eggwash
Black sesame seeds
Coriander leaves

crisped zucchini flowers filled with porcini ricotta

Sweat garlic and shallots in the olive oil. Add porcini mushrooms and thyme and sauté for one minute. Remove from heat and cool.

Roughly chop and mix with ricotta and parmesan in a bowl. Season with freshly cracked black pepper and sea salt.

Place the mixture in a piping bag and fill zucchini flowers, twisting the tips to seal in the stuffing.

Heat enough oil to make a small deep fryer.

Dust the zucchini flowers with plain flour and then dip in the batter.

Fry the zucchini flowers when the oil reaches 170°C (340°F) and drain onto absorbent kitchen paper. Sprinkle with sea salt and serve immediately.

2 garlic cloves, minced
3 shallots, minced
50ml (1¾ fl oz) olive oil
100g (3½oz) porcini mushrooms
1 teaspoon thyme leaves
300g (10oz) fresh ricotta cheese
50g (1½oz) parmesan
Black pepper and sea salt, to taste
10 zucchini flowers
Cottonseed or vegetable oil
½ cup plain flour
1 quantity beer batter (see page 29)

roast duck and pickled mango rice paper rolls

Combine vinegar, sugar, shallots, chilli and garlic in a non-corrosive saucepan and simmer for five minutes.

Peel green mango and cut into strips using a vegetable peeler. Pour the hot pickling mixture over the mango strips. Refrigerate overnight.

Score the skin and fat on the duck breast, seal in a heavy pan and transfer to an oven at 180°C (350°F) for five–seven minutes until medium rare. Rest and cool. Slice the breast into 10, cover and refrigerate.

Cook glass noodles in simmering water for two–three minutes, remove from heat and cool in ice water. Drain well and place in a mixing bowl. Add bean sprouts and lettuce. Toss well and season with ground Szechwan pepper and salt.

Place five rice papers in a bowl of tepid water for about 15 seconds. Remove from the bowl and place on a clean tea towel without any overlapping.

On each rice paper, place a tablespoon of noodle mixture on the bottom quarter. Place a slice of duck breast and some pickled mango on top of the noodles.

Gently roll up to tightly enclose the filling, about halfway. Add a mint leaf and then fold the two sides in and continue to roll up completely. The mint leaf should be visible through the skin.

Repeat the process for the other papers, covering completed wraps with a damp cloth to avoid drying out. Serve with hoisin sauce.

250ml (8 fl oz) white vinegar
100g (3½oz) sugar
2 shallots, chopped
2 birds eye chillies, chopped
2 cloves garlic, chopped
1 green mango
1 large duck breast
100g (3½oz) glass noodles
1 cup bean sprouts
1 cup shredded iceberg lettuce
Szechwan pepper and salt, to taste
10 rice paper wrappers
10 mint leaves
Hoisin sauce, to serve

peppered lamb fillet crostini, truffled mushroom paté

Melt butter in a pan and sweat the garlic and shallots for two minutes without colouring.

Blitz mushrooms in a food processor, scraping down the sides if necessary.

When the mushrooms are minced, add to the pan with thyme and cook over a medium heat for five minutes. Turn the heat to low and cook a further five minutes. Add truffle oil and season with freshly ground black pepper and sea salt.

Very lightly, butter both sides of the croutons and bake at 175°C (350°F) until golden brown.

Roll lamb fillets in a little cracked black pepper and cook in a hot pan with olive oil for four minutes, rolling regularly to cook evenly. Rest for five minutes.

Using a teaspoon, generously mound the mushroom paté on each crouton. Slice the lamb fillets on the angle against the grain, 5mm (¼in) thick. Place a slice on each crouton and serve.

50g (1¾oz) unsalted butter
1 garlic clove, minced
2 shallots, minced
40g (1½oz) Swiss brown mushrooms
½ teaspoon thyme
1 teaspoon truffle oil
Black pepper and sea salt, to taste
2 tablespoons unsalted butter, softened
10 croutons, cut from a ficelle or small baguette
2 lamb fillets
2 tablespoons olive oil

tataki of sashimi tuna, soba noodles, shaved calamari, shiitake mushrooms and snowpeas

Trim tuna so that it is perfectly cylindrical in shape.

Mix sesame seeds together and roll the tuna through the seeds, pressing firmly to imbed.

Heat a non-stick fry pan. When hot, sear the tuna evenly by constantly rolling in the pan. The sesame seeds will toast and the tuna should only be seared to a depth of no more than 2mm (¹⁄₁₆in). Cool and wrap tightly in about four layers of plastic wrap and refrigerate.

In the same pan with a little peanut oil, cook the baby calamari for 45 seconds each side, pressing with a spatula or egg flip during the cooking process. Cool and cut into very fine slivers.

Sauté the shiitakes in a little peanut oil to soften. Julienne the blanched snowpeas.

Whisk together soy, ketchup manis, vinegar, oils, mirin and garlic to make the dressing.

Cook noodles in boiling water and cool quickly under cold running water. Drain well and place in a medium bowl. Add shaved calamari, shiitake mushrooms, snowpeas, coriander and half the dressing. Toss well and share the salad between four plates.

Using a very sharp knife, cut the tuna into 7mm (¼in) thick slices. Remove the plastic wrap and place the tuna on the soba noodle salad. Drizzle each plate with a little extra dressing.

1 barrel-shaped piece of sashimi grade yellowfin tuna (8cm (3in) in length and 5cm (2in) in diameter)
1 teaspoon white sesame seeds
1 teaspoon black sesame seeds
2 tablespoons peanut oil
4 baby calamari, cleaned
8 shiitake mushrooms, cleaned and sliced
12 snowpeas, blanched and refreshed
40ml (1¾ fl oz) soy sauce
40ml (1¾ fl oz) ketchup manis
60ml (2 fl oz) rice vinegar
2 teaspoons sesame oil
2 teaspoons fragrant peanut oil
60ml (2 fl oz) mirin
2 cloves garlic, finely sliced
250g (8oz) dried soba noodles
½ cup coriander leaves, washed and dried

crayfish laksa, teardrop rice noodles, bean shoots and asian herbs

Combine all ingredients from the dried prawns to the coriander seeds in a food processor and blitz to a paste.

Fry the paste in a little oil to release the fragrances. Add coconut milk, bring to the boil and simmer for 10 minutes.

Add stock and simmer a further 10 minutes. Season with fish sauce, lime juice and palm sugar to taste.

Remove tail meat from the crayfish shell and cut into 2cm (¾in) chunks. Remove leg meat from the shell and reserve with the crayfish chunks.

Immerse teardrop rice noodles in boiling water for one minute and then strain.

Warm the crayfish meat in a small pot of simmering laksa. When hot, strain off the cray meat, adding the laksa broth back into the main pot.

Mix bean shoots, Vietnamese mint, coriander leaves, two tablespoons fried shallots and chilli in a bowl.

Divide the rice noodles between four broth bowls. Place a good handful of the bean shoot mix in the centre of each bowl. Share the warmed cray meat between each bowl, arranging around the bean shoots. Ladle the hot laksa broth around the bean shoots to barely cover the cray meat. Garnish with Kaffir lime threads and remaining fried shallots.

2 teaspoons dried prawns, dry roasted
1 teaspoon belacan shrimp paste, dry roasted
1 teaspoon grated fresh turmeric
5cm (2in) piece of galangal, peeled and chopped
3 birds eye chillies
3 coriander roots, washed twice
1 lemongrass stalk, outer layer removed and finely sliced
15 Vietnamese mint leaves
8 Kaffir lime leaves, rib removed
6 red shallots, peeled and sliced
4 garlic cloves, peeled and sliced
30g (1oz) candlenuts
1 teaspoon coriander seeds, roasted and ground
440ml (14½ fl oz) coconut milk
500ml (16 fl oz) light chicken stock
Fish sauce
Lime juice
Palm sugar
1 x 1kg (2lb) freshly cooked whole crayfish
400g (13oz) teardrop rice noodles
100g (3½oz) bean shoots
½ bunch Vietnemese mint, picked
½ bunch coriander, picked
3 tablespoons fried shallots
1 birds eye chilli, seeded and finely sliced
2 Kaffir lime leaves, cut into very fine threads

cassoulet of duck, lyonnaise sausage and white beans

Rinse and cover white beans with water and soak overnight.

Over a low-medium flame, heat duck or goose fat in a saucepan. Add a head of garlic that has been cut in half, rosemary and rock salt. Add half a cup of water and let bubble away for around 15 minutes to flavour the fat.

Add duck legs. Turn stove up to high until the fat returns to a boil. Reduce heat and continue simmering gently for a further 40 minutes, adding 50ml (1¾ fl oz) of water every 10 minutes when you think the previous water may have evaporated. The water will stop the fat from frying and drying out the duck meat.

Remove duck legs from the fat and cool. Strain the fat and refrigerate for future use.

Sweat onion in olive oil for three minutes until softened but not coloured. Add thyme and drained white beans and cover with chicken stock. Simmer until the beans are almost cooked and the chicken stock has been absorbed. Stir very gently during this process.

Render lardons for three minutes in a pan over medium heat, tossing regularly.

Cut the duck legs in half through the leg joint. Add the halved duck legs, crisped lardons and Lyonnaise sausage to the white beans.

Add veal stock and bring cassoulet back to a very gentle simmer for 10 minutes. Do not boil the cassoulet as it will break up the beans and become cloudy.

Adjust seasoning to taste and serve.

200g (6½oz) dried white beans
800g (1½lb) duck or goose fat
1 head of garlic
4 branches rosemary
1 tablespoon rock salt
4 large duck legs
1 large brown onion, cut into 1cm (⅜in) dice
3 tablespoons olive oil
6 sprigs thyme
Chicken stock, to cover
2cm (¾in) slab of smoked pork belly, cut into lardons
400g (13oz) Lyonnaise sausage, cut into large chunks
1L (32 fl oz) reduced brown veal stock

Andrew Blake is one of Melbourne's favourite chefs. Over the past 30 years, Andrew's expertise and creative abilities have earned him high praise and many industry awards, including a lifetime achievement award from *The Age Good Food Guide*.

Andrew's primary experience is in running successful restaurants, including his restaurant Blake's at Southgate throughout the 1990s. Andrew transferred his focus to catering in response to a strong demand for restaurant-quality food in any environment; which proves challenging at times, but extremely satisfying.